The Red Pill Executive

ENDORSEMENTS

Simple is hard. Complexity is easy. *The Red Pill Executive* takes a complicated topic and turns it into a simple and easy read that's so deep it merits reading again and again. The authors set the bar high and then deliver practical steps coming from their years of experience in the field.

They also fearlessly confront culture. In a previous position, I experienced the power of culture while on a team tasked with making a radical shift toward more accountability. Two years in, we had a cultural snap-back where morale and loyalty fell apart to the point that we had a downturn in customer satisfaction. The book's case study on this topic felt like someone was a fly on the wall in my office back then. I wish I had read that chapter years ago.

> These guys must have watched a movie of the last 10 years of my professional life!

Anyone working with projects should have a copy of *The Red Pill Executive* on their office shelf. You'll read about creating successful PM teams, for sure, but you'll also get insights on safely navigating company culture, and you might even learn how to be more effective yourself.

~**Steve Jenkins**, Global Program Management Leader,
Large Aerospace Company

I love the way that *The Red Pill Executive* articulates what the seasoned professional intuitively knows about how to navigate culture and the efficacy that carries with it. It provides a framework and gives clarity to something that is felt at a gut level and learned through experience. Their explanation also gave me tools that will help me train my teams to understand culture in a way that makes sense in the day-to-day operations of projects.

> "...a marvelous mix of research, experience and storytelling."

The authors' use of movies makes it a marvelous mix of research, experience, and storytelling. Weaving the concepts through action movies is a brilliant way to illustrate the paradigm shift in thinking that takes place when we look at culture as a core component of managing change. It also made the read enjoyable as well as practical.

I wish I could say it was a quick read, but I stopped to mark up my copy with notes so frequently that it took me a while to get through it. I sat down to read and ended up captured by the ideas. I'll return to those notes many, many times. Bottom line, this book made me want to work with the guys at Think!

~**Kate Krupey**, Technology Executive Advisor, former CIO of KatzAbosch, P.A.

THE
RED PILL
EXECUTIVE

TRANSFORM OPERATIONS AND UNLOCK
THE POTENTIAL OF CORPORATE CULTURE

**TONY
GRUEBL**

**JEFF
WELCH**

**BRYAN
WOLBERT**

NEW YORK

LONDON • NASHVILLE • MELBOURNE • VANCOUVER

The Red Pill Executive

Transform Operations and Unlock the Potential of Corporate Culture

Published in New York, New York, by Morgan James Publishing. Morgan James is a trademark of Morgan James, LLC. www.MorganJamesPublishing.com

ISBN 9781642799491 paperback
ISBN 9781642799507 eBook
Library of Congress Control Number: 2019956188

Cover Design by:
Christopher Kirk
www.GFSstudio.com

Interior Design by:
Chris Treccani
www.3dogcreative.net

Morgan James is a proud partner of Habitat for Humanity Peninsula and Greater Williamsburg. Partners in building since 2006.

Get involved today! Visit
MorganJamesPublishing.com/giving-back

TABLE OF CONTENTS

Foreword   xv
Acknowledgments   xvii
Preface   xix

Introduction   **xxiii**
    A Different Playbook   xxv
    Failure is Baked In   xxvi
    Scaling the Project Management Model   xxvii
    The Missing Element   xxviii

Chapter 1   **Why Project Management Fails a Whopping 70% of the Time**   **1**
    Cool Tools but Worse Results   3
    Who's in Charge Here?   4
    Pointing Fingers   5
    Taking Ownership   7
    Case Study:
    USVantage: A Company President Walled in by their Operations Culture   8
    Trap of the Iron Triangle   10
    Chapter 1 Summary   11

Chapter 2	**What Does It Take to Win?**	**17**
	Measuring Business Value	18
	Measuring Strategic Alignment	19
	The Human Element	22
	Strategic Alignment and Executive Alignment	26
	Choosing the Red Pill	33
	Chapter 2 Summary	34
Chapter 3	**Taking Off the Gloves**	**37**
	Embrace Your Feelings	42
	Own It	44
	Rapid Immersion and Control	45
	Test for Risks	46
	Example: Sending Jimmie for Coffee	47
	Focus Teams	49
	The Three-Sided Table	50
	Chapter 3 Summary	51
Chapter 4	**Finding Red Pill Recruits**	**57**
	How Personality Affects Recruit Success	60
	Operating in the BKPM Resting Zone	66
	Core Traits of the Natural	69
	Unafraid of Conflict and Confrontation	69
	Simple, Direct, and Effective	70
	Disciplined	70
	Well-Trained and Versatile	71
	Moves Forward Consistently	72
	The Red Pill Attitude	72
	Chapter 4 Summary	73
Chapter 5	**Rewiring the System**	**77**
	The Neuroscience Behind It	79
	The Hand Model of the Brain	80

Julie   82
A Very Smart Man   82
Bat and Ball   83
The Myth of Multitasking   85
Example: Analysis Paralysis   86
Example: Looking for an Exit, any Exit!   87
The Red Pill and Limbic Learning   87
Creating Lasting Change   89
Example: Taking the Fight to the Back Lot   93
Chapter 5 Summary   94

Chapter 6   **The Currency of Effectiveness**   **97**
A New Look at The Iron Triangle   99
A New Perspective on Challenge   101
Strategic Alignment: Business Purpose meets Project
Mastery   103
Case Study: MIRA: An organization with a time
management problem.   104
Finding Strategic Alignment   107
Taking Effectiveness to the Next Level: Scalability   110
Rapid Control Process   111
Chapter 6 Summary   112

Chapter 7   **Spreading the Red Pill Mindset**   **117**
Stage 1: The Red Pill Operative Becomes a Sage   118
Case Study: Mardia, A Company Who Thought the Red
Pill Was a Great Idea   120
Case Study: A Company Wanting Red Pill Results While
Keeping Their Blue Pill Mindset   121
Culture + Business Value = Effectiveness   123
Stage 2: Organic Change   125
Stage 3: An Informal Red Pill Alliance Forms   126
Case Study: Seeding for Change   128

A Case for Patience 131

Case Study: A Startup in Forced Growth 132

Stage 4: The Bare Knuckled Organization Becomes a Red Pill PMO 133

Chapter 7 Summary 134

Chapter 8   **The Indigenous Bare Knuckled Organization**   **135**

Case Study: Epilogue from Seeding for Change 136

Case Study: More from "We Learned a Lot" 138

Red Pill Operations Face More Challenges 139

Creating an Informal Bare Knuckled Organization 142

Case Study: Pro-Fit—A Bare Knuckled Organization Emerges During Massive Expansion 142

Chapter 8 Summary 142

Chapter 9   **The Secret Ingredient**   **151**

Red Pill or blue pill: Which are you? 157

Beware the Blue Pill Red Herring 160

Case Study: Executive with Silos 162

An Ancient Allegory 164

The Emergence of a Red Pill Organization 168

The Gift In The Battle 170

Chapter 9 Summary 171

Chapter 10   **Throw Out Your Old Yardstick**   **173**

Derailed Purpose 177

A New Yardstick 178

States of Culture 179

Benefits of Culture-Currents and Resistance 183

Deploying the Power of Culture 185

Three Approaches to Dealing with Cultural Change 186

1. More Change Faster 186

Case Study: Research Campus 186

2. Less Change Slower But With Persistence   188
Case Study: Green Tech Company   188
3. Violent, Rapid Change   190
Case Study: Epilogue to "We Learned a Lot"   190
Not A Quick Fix   191
What If You Knew You Couldn't Lose?   193
Chapter 10 Summary   194

About the Authors   197
Glossary   199
Resources   201
Endnotes   207

FOREWORD

When I first learned about Think Systems, I was CTO during a merger that had all the earmarks of a first-class disaster. We were two years in. The situation was becoming more and more complex, and our deadline was only three months away.

I'm a transformational agilest, and I had tried to address the project using agile methods. I had a great team with stellar business analysts, developers, scrum masters, user experience architects, and more. However, this project had gaps, and throwing more developers or business analysts at it would only be adding resources to areas that weren't really the problem.

Just as an example, say I had people who could write great user stories, but those great writers had no concept of how to tailor those stories to highlight our competitive advantage. Those talented writers were actually blockers because they didn't deliver the value we needed. By realizing the problem and opening up those blocks, the rest of the team could finally make progress.

I needed someone to find the blocks in the merger and help us open them up.

That's when I called in Think. They gave us a Strategic Project Manager and two full-time PMs as well as several others. Basically, they landed on us like the Marines storming a beach. What happened after that blew me away. We finished the merger before the three-month deadline and did it with elegance.

Seeing how they handled that dire situation, I learned how to modify my own approach to my teams. I placed less weight on certifications and more weight on the conduct of the individual. PMs who wanted to follow formulas simply for the sake of following formulas didn't cut it anymore. Now I was looking for team members who understood what it meant to be in alignment with the company vision and mission. I wanted someone who knew the meaning of Business Value Potential and who had the courage speak out when they saw a block looming ahead.

I wanted someone who had more than simple technical know-how. I wanted someone who understood culture, who had a sense of what makes the key players tick, and who had some personal investment in the outcome. I wanted someone who could build a strategy based on solid principles, but with the flexibility to match the specific situation so we could make real progress that mattered.

Think changed my entire perspective on what effective project management entailed. However, at the same time I also realized that the amount of manpower and time they had invested in our company meant their process was not scalable. They'd have to train several teams filled with capable, savvy operators like Tony, Bryan, and others who were willing to work hard and long to get the job done.

Over the years since then, I've seen these brilliant professionals go through a maturing process. They actually cracked the code. Not only have they scaled their process, but they've broken the steps down into a readable, informative, and entertaining (albeit somewhat in-your-face) book.

Fasten your seatbelt. Things are about to get real when you dig into this stuff. These guys don't mince words, and they don't take prisoners. You're gonna love 'em.

John Camp
Technology Executive Advisor, former CTO of Bloomberg BNA, Lippincott Williams and Wilkins, Wolters Kluwer Health Division, and Sheshunoff Information Services, Thomson Financial Media Group

ACKNOWLEDGMENTS

Thank you to those who encourage us to question everything to get better at what we do! Without Lana McAra, our amazingly creative and talented collaborator and Ghost Writer, this book would otherwise be dry and poorly written in the voice of three guys in a Baltimore bar, telling stories about how our profession is like the movie Pulp Fiction. Lana is the best-selling, award-winning author of more than 20 titles and she's a sought-after speaker. She made this book interesting and fun to write and generally tolerated our shenanigans.

Each of the coauthors have families and friends who allowed us to drone on endlessly about frameworks and observations shared in this book. They include wives, kids, mothers, fathers, best friends, and old and new acquaintances. Your kind smiles and attempts to really understand our world kept us moving forward.

Many thanks to those who edited, read, commented, criticized, admonished, laughed at, and sometimes agreed with the content in these pages. There are too many to name all, but a special thanks goes to present and past Think team members, Dale Matthews, John Camp, Dan Kuffer, Ed Mullin, Ed Hale, Scott Klinger, Erica McQuiston, Scott Sax, Kevin Palmer, Miguel Buddle, Katrina Kastendieck, Ben Adrian, Jewel Green, Andrew Mavronicolas, Rick Thomas, John Hill, Joe Miller, and Sharon Gibala-Marsh, and colleagues, Steve Jenkins, Professor Jim Kucher, Mike Karfakis (and the great team at Vitamin), Collin Cohen, Bill Collier, and

Michael Dobson, and photographer Nick Gruebl, and proofreader Mary Coddington.

Finally, thank you to Morgan James Publishing for their support, coaching, and professionalism in bringing this book to market.

Inspired by the legend, Domine Quo Vadis.

PREFACE

2018 statistics show that Operations initiatives—for simplicity we call them *projects*—come to a less-than-desirable outcome 70% of the time.[1] If you are an Operations Executive, at the end of a project you're sure to wind up in front of a boardroom trying to come up with an explanation for what went wrong. If you've been in Operations for any time at all, you've been there more often than you'd like to think about. If you're new to Operations, you're on a slippery slope, my friend.

Fortunately for you, you have an edge. You picked up this book. We've been managing operations for more than 16 years, and we refused to resign ourselves to failure more than two-thirds of the time.

> "Here lies the body of Mary Lee; died at the age of a hundred and three. For fifteen years she kept her virginity; not a bad record for this vicinity."
>
> **– Captain Quint in Jaws**[98]

The Matrix[2]
Starring Keanu Reeves and Laurence Fishburne
Warner Bros Pictures (1999)

In *The Matrix*, Keanu Reeves plays a man leading a double life. By day he is a software developer, by night he

---

is Neo, a high-level hacker. He receives a cryptic message on his computer screen from the legendary hacker named Morpheus (Laurence Fishburne), followed by a knock on the door. Several people stand outside waiting to lead him to Morpheus.

Morpheus explains to Neo that humans exist in a false reality constructed to hide the truth. This false world is known as The Matrix. Everyone in The Matrix is a slave, sleepwalking through life, simply following the *status quo* with no hope for a better way, pawns to others with self-serving agendas.

Morpheus holds out his two hands. In each is a pill: in his left palm is a blue pill, in his right is a red pill. If Neo takes the blue pill, he will wake up in his bed and "believe whatever you want to believe." But if he takes the red pill, his eyes will open. He'll know what's truly going on in the world.

Neo takes the red pill.

Immediately he sees the world in a completely different way. He asks Morpheus, "Can I go back?" to which Morpheus replies, "No."

The red-pill blue-pill scene from *The Matrix* is a part of pop culture now. It represents the paradox of choice. If we choose to, we can see things differently, but we must make a conscious and deliberate choice. We took an honest look at the blue-pill Project Management model in today's world and turned it inside out. We pulled off our gloves and got our hands dirty. We took the fight to the back lot. We kicked butt and took names. What we learned is radical, unsettling, and even scary for some.

This book is much more about effectiveness and how to achieve more of it than project management. Over the years, we formulated and refined our Red Pill model, chipping away at our own preconditioning and squashing our assumptions. Our goal: to determine how each company's culture measures and cultivates effectiveness and how to reach the maximum velocity that culture will allow.

- We debunked mythologies.
- We moved the spotlight to what really matters.
- We measured twice and cut once.
- We deconstructed complicated systems and replaced them with simple principles.
- We reworked a stuffy, cumbersome model and transformed it into something alive, effective, and rewarding.

Our initiatives scored in at a better than 95% success rate.

In 2013, we released our findings and published <u>Bare Knuckled Project Management</u>. As a result, thousands of operators took the red pill. The concept caught on. Our red-pill model began to transform Operations within our client organizations. Operations Executives who embraced this shift in perspective saw their own performance ratings rise while the C-suite looked on, wondering about their secret formula.

That formula is in your hands right now.

If you're in Operations—veteran or rookie—you're in the right place. If you're a project manager, you're in the right place. Just be aware, before this ride is over, you'll come face to face with a choice: red pill or blue. The rest is up to you.

> "Our goal: to determine how each company's culture measures and cultivates effectiveness and how to reach the maximum velocity that culture will allow."

INTRODUCTION

Year after year, the Project Management Institute and The Standish Group have consistently reported the massive failure rates of company projects. This year, the chance of success is 30%. That's a total or partial failure rate of 70%. What's even more surprising is that the numbers held fairly steady at 68% failure for about 10 years, then ramped up to 71% in 2015[3] and then settled at 70% in 2018. We have more tools at our fingertips than ever before, but things continue to get worse instead of better.

> "Nothing is wrong here. Especially near the nuclear reactor."
>
> **~Gilda Radner**
> **as Roseanne**
> **Roseannadanna,**
> *Saturday Night Live*[99]

- 17% of IT initiatives go so badly they can threaten the very existence of the company."[4]
- 73% of those surveyed admit their ventures are always or usually doomed from the start.[5]
- Failed IT projects cost the US economy about $50-150 billion annually.[6]
- Organizations waste $109 million for every US $1 billion invested.[7]

Project success rates went from 16% in 1994 to 28% in 2000, up to 32% by 2013, back to 29% in 2016[8] and up to 30% in 2018.[9]

> ### *Jaws*[10]
> Starring Roy Scheider, Robert Shaw, and Richard Dreyfuss
> Zanuck/Brown Productions (1975)
>
> During a hot summer in a small beach community, the new Sheriff Martin Brody (Roy Scheider) discovers a shark attack victim on the beach. He wants to close the beaches, but local businessmen resist. Brody backs down, and a young boy falls victim to the predator. When the grieving mother announces a bounty on the shark, amateur shark hunters and fisherman swarm into town, hoping to land the reward.
>
> The beaches remain open, and the death toll rises.
>
> At a town meeting, an experienced shark hunter named Capt. Quint (Robert Shaw) offers to hunt down the shark for an exorbitant price. Soon Quint, Brody, and marine biologist Matt Hooper (Richard Dreyfuss) are at sea, hunting the Great White Shark. As Brody succinctly surmises after their first encounter with the giant creature, they're going to need a bigger boat.[11]

In the classic Steven Spielberg movie, *Jaws,* a ravenous Great White Shark gets a taste for tourists in a small beach town. With the death toll rising rapidly, Sheriff Brody becomes an operations executive with one clear goal—to take out the shark. Brody assembles a team of operators—a marine biologist named Matt Hooper and an eccentric boat captain named Quint.

If Brody were a typical blue-pill operator, the shark would have a 70% chance of winning. Our question: Why?

Why does the average Operations Executive shrug off these horrific stats when their own performance ratings are also in question?

Why do talented, capable Project Management professionals and even Project Management Organizations (PMOs) fail so often?

Why isn't someone asking the right questions and coming up with better answers?

"Why isn't someone asking the right questions and coming up with better answers?"

A Different Playbook

On April 26, 1986, the Soviet Union's Chernobyl nuclear power station exploded, releasing more than 50 tons of radioactive material into the atmosphere. It was the worst nuclear power plant accident in history. Always concerned about negative press, the Soviets attempted a cover up. Two days later, Swedish radiation monitoring stations more than 800 miles away reported radiation levels 40% higher than normal. After a string of denials, the Soviet news agency finally acknowledged that a major nuclear accident had indeed occurred at Chernobyl.[12]

To the Soviets, damage control with the media was their first priority. Our safety-conscious Western minds saw this as beyond ludicrous. So did the writers at *Saturday Night Live*. In a classic SNL skit a few weeks later, actor Gilda Radner played a Russian news reporter in Chernobyl saying, "Nothing is wrong here. Especially near the nuclear reactor."[13]

"The Soviets saw their actions as perfectly logical. They just had a different playbook."

Whether we understand them or not, the Soviets saw their actions as perfectly logical. They just had a different playbook.

Could the blue-pill Project Management model have its own playbook? Why else would such an inefficient system continue for decades without a major overhaul?

This is business where numbers rule. We started to wonder if we were looking at the wrong numbers.

Failure is Baked In[14]

Most executives claim their Operations run fairly well. Always room for improvement, mind you, but overall their projects deliver what they need to keep their company running and profitable.

That's right. Everything's fine with projects.

Except it isn't.

Imagine taking your car to a repair shop who gives you a quote and a timeframe. When you arrive to pick it up, the car isn't ready and won't be ready for a while. The repair takes twice as long and costs three times as much as your quote. You drive off the lot with the engine clanging and smoke trailing from the exhaust pipe. When your friend asks how you like your repair shop, you nonchalantly reply, "They do fairly well."

> "You knew there was a shark out there! You knew it was dangerous! But you let people go swimming anyway?"
>
> ~Mrs. Kintner in Jaws[100]

Really?

Perceptions are tricky. Human beings have a natural inclination to make offhanded statements with little evidence to back them up. For blue-pill managers, it's often easier to say, "Nothing is wrong here. Especially near the nuclear reactor."

While an expectation of failure might seem absurd, it does make sense when you consider project success rates stayed at 32% for about 10 years, then dipped to 29% in 2015[15] and improved by a meager 1% more by 2018. And this despite new support organizations, new tools and processes, and the new concept of the Project Management Organization [PMO].

When failure is the norm, leaders naturally end up thinking: *Sure, projects fail. They always have, and they always will. Maybe we just need to deal with it.* They repeat truisms like, "Take your worst estimate and double it."[16]

With the odds so heavily in the shark's favor. Sooner or later, every blue-pill operative will fall into the 38% or the 33% range. Count on it. If you're the one in charge, those numbers also affect you.

We of the red-pill persuasion maintain that consistent success is not only possible, it's practical and attainable. Our 95% success rate backs us up.

> "Everything hinges on leaders who have the *cojones* to take the red pill and open their eyes."

When Red Pill executives know how to develop and lead a Red Pill team, their success will draw attention, and others will want in on the action. That's when things go viral.

Everything hinges on leaders who have the *cojones* to take the red pill and open their eyes.

Scaling the Project Management Model

A PMO is a living organism made up of people, processes, and projects. PMO members represent a collective treasury of wisdom, skill, knowledge, and experience. They work in many disciplines within a single department or across the entire company. Many mid-size companies see a PMO as a necessary part of doing business. Smaller companies and startups have *ad hoc* teams to execute their change initiatives without organizing an official PMO. When we use the term PMO, we refer to both groups.

How well do PMOs perform?

According to the self-reporting model in "The State of the PMO 2016"[17], current PMOs are doing just fine. In this survey, 226 respondents report that 85% of corporations have a PMO, and most PMOs report directly to a C-level executive inside the company. The study cites numerous statistics to show a direct correlation between the maturity of a company's PMO and the value it provides. According to them, mature PMOs are far more likely to meet critical success factors. They also show improvements in cost savings per project, better schedule and budget performance, and greater productivity, with fewer failed projects.[18]

Maturity does make a difference. Consider the performance gap between a fledgling salesperson vs. a seasoned pro. The rookie memorizes scripts, practices gestures, and beefs up on body language. The pro leads an instinctive sales dance that comes from the core. That's what maturity does. However, if the pro has a faulty foundation—a.k.a. blue-pill perspective—no amount of experience will take him to real success.

> "Self-reporting has this fallacy built in. Imagine what Chernobyl experts would say when self-reporting on their performance."

Comparing himself with his rookie coworker, the pro sees himself as stellar. However, in the broader scope of things he's still stuck at the 70% fail rate like other blue pill sales pros.

Self-reporting has this fallacy built in. Imagine what Chernobyl experts would say when self-reporting on their performance.

Statistics show blue-pill PMOs might excel at completing processes, such as writing project plans and filling out reports, but they still have a 70% overall failure rate.[19] Despite these numbers, the "State of the PMO" survey makes it clear that PMOs and Operations Executives value their company's PMO and are generally very satisfied with the results.[20]

Even scaled up, the attitude remains the same: "Nothing is wrong here. Especially near the nuclear reactor."

The Missing Element

Consider the Sydney Opera House which took 15 years to build and ended up 14 times over budget. That structure has a global reputation as an engineering masterpiece. Can we call it a failure? The Opera House is a great example to show that the triple constraints of time, cost, and scope are not the only criteria to determine success. Other criteria come into play.[21]

After years of research, we found a hidden marker in every project. Whether or not the Operations Executive or project manager is aware of them, each initiative has an additional objective besides completing the task: adding value to the business.

Yet, most operations teams, both *ad hoc* and PMO, ignore the importance of Business Value. Only half of survey responders said their

PMO includes Business Value in any reports. Less than a third had objective analysis to quantify their Business Value.[22]

According to "The State of the PMO 2010":

> "Each project has an additional objective besides completing the task: adding value to the business."

> In our experience, not everyone measures business value. But of those in this research that do, 31% report a decrease in failed projects, 30% report projects delivered under budget; 21% report improvements in productivity; 19% report projects delivered ahead of schedule and 17% report cost savings … an average of US $567,000 per project.[23]

Red pill Operations Executives consistently keep Business Value in front of their teams. Success involves much more than meeting the requirements of The Triple Constraint Model—time, budget, and performance (also known as "The Iron Triangle" because of its rigidity). However, only those who swallow the red pill can see that.

To meet both goals—completing the task and adding value to the business—Red Pill operators take ownership to a new level. They view each new project as an entrepreneurial endeavor, and they are in it to win it.

They fill their team with people who can fix problems, improve their business at many levels, and get projects done effectively. No more wasted time and money on initiatives that should never happen or that fail because they weren't properly developed or executed.

They get clear on every objective, take charge, and create a plan that gets the job done with real world results. They lead their team into battle fully loaded and hyper-ready.

No more ticking off check boxes and idling, waiting for 5:00.

No more passing the buck or saying, "It's not my problem."

No more jaded apathy.

When they take the red pill, their eyes open wide. These leaders aren't in this position to fill a cubicle. They're here to get stuff done. Initiatives exist to produce Business Value.

These operators go into Value Capture Mode and make decisions with value as their primary criteria. They understand the project's strategic implications for reaching the company's mission and help everyone involved to keep their eye on the ball. As new information comes in, the scope and constraints of the project shift like an underwater plant, rooted in the ground but swaying with the currents.

> "Initiatives exist to produce Business Value."

Now the project aligns with broader company goals. That's the sweet spot where success happens. It's quantifiable and repeatable. It's a game changer and career maker.

However, make no mistake. Taking the red pill is not for the fainthearted.

Taking the red pill means full out commitment. Taking the red pill means you pull off the gloves and get your hands dirty. Taking the red pill means you kick butt and take names.

We're here to show you how.

CHAPTER 1

Why Project Management Fails a Whopping 70% of the Time

"It's a new day, people. Destiny Calls. The world expects only one thing from us. That we will win."

~Master Sergeant Farell in Edge of Tomorrow[24]

Edge of Tomorrow[25]
Starring Tom Cruise and Emily Blunt
Warner Bros Pictures (2014)

When attacked by an alien force, the best military units in the world working together can't seem to beat them. Tom Cruise plays Major William Cage, a Public Relations officer with no combat experience who finds himself on a suicide mission.

> The enemy came in the form of black shape-shifting Mimics that hide under the sand, an octopus-type thing that rolls like a tumbleweed. It had claws on each of its many legs and a gaping dragon mouth. These Mimics had two forms: the orange warrior and the powerful blue Alpha. The blue Alpha monitored battlefield events to learn the opponent's strategy, then reset time while preserving memory. This gave the aliens an unstoppable advantage.
>
> Within minutes of landing on a beach battlefront resembling WWII's Normandy invasion, Cage blows up a blue Alpha as it attacks him. Covered with Alpha blood, Cage dies. He then enters a time loop, living out the same brutal day, fighting and dying again and again.
>
> This time loop gives Cage the chance to improve his combat skills and his understanding of the enemy. He soon teams up with Special Forces warrior Sergeant Rita Vrtaski (Emily Blunt). Working together, they learn what it means to win at something that seems unbeatable.

Watching patterns of human behavior, we often see the human response of "doing the same thing over and over again but expecting different results."[26] This is so common it has become a cliché in folklore, music, books, and movies—essentially anything that embodies culture. Managing this response and creating a new outcome is at the core of almost every business book and methodology ever developed.

Edge of Tomorrow is a marvelous example of this repetition-response situation very similar to the 70% project failure rate. Many before us have tried to win using cool tools and new plans. They've spent millions on developing highly specialized software and intensive training. Yet the failure rate continues to creep upward. What was a 68% fail rate in 2015, has now climbed to 70%.

In the movie, after hundreds of attempts Cage always had the same result. He died, and the armies of Earth went down in defeat. According to McKinsey.com, "17% of IT projects go so bad that they can threaten the very existence of the company."

> "17% of IT projects go so bad that they can threaten the very existence of the company.[101]"

In our own quest, we refused to sit back with the blue-pill attitude of "that's just the way things are." Bit by bit, over time, we tried various tactics and strategies, found what worked, and pressed ahead to the next challenge eager to learn more.

Some of our clients welcomed our new approach with open arms. They allowed us to test our mettle in the field. Others resisted. Their pushback shocked us into reality when we were inadvertently drinking our own Kool-Aid˚.

Cool Tools but Worse Results

Over the past 20 years, project management tools have improved every year with promises of more productivity, faster, and better than ever before. We'd have a hard time keeping up with the increasing complexity without these advances. Nobody is disputing that.

We have the Project Management Institute (PMI˚) with their *PM Book of Knowledge* (PMBOK). We have thousands of certified Project Management professionals.

We have Microsoft˚ SharePoint for central documentation, Microsoft˚ Project, SmartSheet˚ and hundreds of other online tools.

We have Jira˚, VersionOne˚, and CA Agile Central˚ for technical teams, Microsoft˚ Excel with embedded Business Intelligence tools for analysis and active management.

We have collaboration tools like WebEx˚, GoToMeeting˚, Zoom˚, and Teams˚ (formerly Skype for Business˚) to keep teams in sync because now we often work virtually.

We have agile development philosophy and frameworks, scrum, SAFe, and others.

Every year PMI* brilliantly updates the *PM Book of Knowledge*. Every year updated tools with better features appear on the market. We are gloriously awash in tools and science with so much more going for us than 10 years ago.

All we have to do is learn the science, and we can turn the odds to our favor, right?

Uhh, not really. Despite all these technical advantages, our success rates continue falling. What is worse, many projects that make it into the success column don't add Business Value to the company.

In *Edge of Tomorrow*, Cage had the most intricate weaponized armor imaginable. He had machine guns strapped to both arms and two rocket launchers on his back. He had state-of-the-art sensors, and a computerized voice feeding him instructions. His armor gave him superhuman strength, including the ability to jump out of an aircraft and land on his feet unharmed. He could push cars out of the way with his hands. Millions went into every high-tech suit, but he still died in the sand.

Like Cage, we also continue to die on the beach. We might reach further inland, but we still fall to cunning Mimics hidden in the sand 70% of the time.

Despite these horrific odds, we knew in our souls that we could win at this game of Project Management. Failure wasn't an option. For Cage, the Alpha Mimic's blood brought him into a special awareness and the time loop. For us, we returned to the *Matrix* metaphor. We summoned all of our courage to step out of the herd and open our eyes.

We took the red pill.

Who's in Charge Here?

The science is good. The tools are great. So, what are the common factors across all operations, in all disciplines, using all tools and development processes? First, it's people. For all their tremendous advances, people are, after all, still human with very specific behaviors dating back to

"You control the power now."[102]

~Sergeant Rita Vrtaski
in *Edge of Tomorrow*

the beginning of humanity. We became curious about psychology and behaviors that could make highly trained and capable professionals a part of the problem.

We looked at The CHAOS Ten[27], the top 10 reasons projects fail, but—to be honest—they read like a list of poor excuses, like "The dog ate my homework."

- It's not our fault.
- It must be the fault of Operations and PMOs.
- The team is incompetent or the project manager doesn't have the right experience.

As a leader, if that's the case, should an initiative go forward at all?

Pointing Fingers

In January 2014, several large Affordable Care Act health exchanges failed. Shortly afterward, writer Kyle Dowling interviewed Dr. Harold Kerzner for a *Huffington Post* blog entitled, "Surviving Disasters in Project Management."[28]

Harold Kerzner, Ph.D., M.S., M.B.A., is Senior Executive Director with International Institute for Learning, Inc. Dr. Kerzner is globally recognized as an expert on project, program, and portfolio management, as well as total quality management. He is a strategic planning expert and the author of over 140 books on engineering and project management, some of them bestsellers.[29] Clearly, Dr. Kerzner is an expert. His experience in all types of endeavors have given him the title, Godfather of Project Management.

In the interview, Kyle Dowling asked Dr. Kerzner the following question: "In your opinion, why has project management been so controversial over the years in terms of its validity as a profession?"

10 Reasons for Project Management Failure from CHAOS:[30]
- Executive support
- User involvement

- Experienced project manager
- Clear business objectives
- Minimized scope
- Standard software infrastructure
- Firm basic requirements
- Formal methodology
- Reliable estimates

Other criteria: small milestones, proper planning, competent staff, and ownership

Dr. Kerzner replied, "My personal belief is that the resistance sits at the senior-most level of management."

That's Number 1 on The CHAOS Ten list: Executive Support.

Dr. Kerzner continued, "They're afraid if they make project management a career path they will have to give the project managers authority and the right to make decisions. They'll essentially have to empower them."

That's Ownership, last in the list under Number 10: Other Criteria.

He further added, "What they're afraid of is that project managers will make decisions that should have been made at the executive level. They resist making it a career path and believe PM can be managed on a part-time basis, which doesn't work."

That one didn't make The CHAOS Ten. Perhaps it is included in "Other" or perhaps it ties to Number 3 related to the experience of the project manager.

Dr. Kerzner went on, "What I'm really saying is that information is power. Those who have control of that information are hesitant about sharing it with project managers, and those who have authority do not want to share that with project managers as well. It has been the stumbling block all along."

Furthermore, Dr. Kerzner attributes the failure of the health insurance exchanges under the Patient Protection and Affordable Care Act to this fundamental problem in project management. It's almost as if he said,

"Dear fellow project managers, we brought down Obama Care. I'm sorry to say."

Is the average Operations Executive really that protective? Do they withhold information and authority from their managers to protect their own executive power... even at the expense of project success? If that's truly the case, withholding information would certainly have significant impact on the 70% failure rate.

Did Dr. Kerzner put his finger on the problem, though? Do Operations Executives truly refuse to empower project managers? Or did Dr. Kerzner examine the symptoms perfectly, yet misdiagnose the problem?

We would say if an initiative has merit, none of these above reasons should exist long enough to derail it. Taking it one step further, the root of the issue lies hidden under Number 10: Other Criteria. Isn't it interesting that the core problem didn't even make The CHAOS Ten list? Instead, it's last in the tacked-on string under Other Criteria: Ownership.

Taking Ownership

One of our authors, Tony Gruebl, started out in Business Intelligence, a difficult field since data always bring up more questions. Even after the best delivery, the customer always wanted more information and was never completely satisfied. The quest for information is unending.

Using the most applauded project management training available, Tony climbed the ranks in the industry. Years later, he did a long-term review of his customers, businesses he had served in good faith with the best intentions and thousands of hours of hard work. What he found was a field of carnage. Many of his customers didn't use their software at all. Many were so frustrated with implementation, they wouldn't use the firm again. One was suing the company.

Dismayed, Tony realized he had been dying on the beach again and again and didn't know it. If he hadn't looked back, he would have never known it.

When Tony launched Think Systems, Inc. (simply called "Think"), he tried a different tactic and went into intensive training to learn another ideology about project management. He learned 5/9 improvement, root cause analysis, and how to make a difference. He mastered important concepts, but at the end of the day that approach still didn't move the needle.

Our greatest asset at that time was putting away our own assumptions and opening our mindset. That was tough, but we could not settle for mediocrity. We took the red pill and opened to a new perspective—taking 100% ownership, no matter what the obstacles or circumstances. That meant brutal honesty, even if it meant getting fired from a particular endeavor.

We learned how to deliver bad news to the sponsor in a way that's empathetic to their needs, so the conversation builds trust into the relationship. Over the years, our process improved until we reached a success rate of 95%. However, even with that rate of success, some sponsors were so enmeshed in company culture and so used to their dismal results that they weren't interested in red pills, even in a crisis.

Case Study:
USVantage: A Company President Walled in by their Operations Culture

Early in Think's history, the president of USVantage brought us in for a critical product launch, a bonded insurance offering that would make a significant addition to their portfolio. We had the president's firm directive that this project must not fail.

Think's team went to work, but soon ran into difficulty. We requested a schedule from Operations and got the response: "We're agile, and we don't work that way."

Team leaders said, "We need to set expectations for customers."

The response was the same: "We're agile, and we don't work that way. Check with someone else."

We found ourselves moving from office to office and getting the same response. We could not implement the project.

This shop stiff armed our team, corporate operations people, the sales team, and everyone else who approached them. Finally, the problem escalated to the president.

He went ape!

Still that shop would not relent. Their culture rewarded obedience to standard practices more than project success.

Eventually, Think's team had to withdraw. This was a cultural issue where one sector of the company had everything locked down.

That client provided tremendous learning for our team. Since then, based on what we observe in our initial contacts, we design a unique plan of action for each client. Now, we'd go after the logjam and design an approach to break it from Day 1.

In *Edge of Tomorrow*[31], when Cage first came awake inside the time loop, he stayed true to his training and allowed Master Sergeant Farell to have control. That's when he realized this approach had only one ending—a swift death on the beach. Before long, Cage's attitude and body language changed. He spoke with authority, became pre-emptive, and assumed responsibility.

He took ownership.

His fellow squad members naturally followed him. Master Sergeant Farell felt confusion as his domineering energy collapsed, but he had no way to fight back.

In the project management world, the Operations Executive who takes ownership for a project's success will see their numbers rise. Working in partnership with a skilled project manager is important, but this is a partnership where information flows easily back and forth, where everyone has a voice. The Operations Executive is always aware and involved in the project with the firm goal of seeing it completed well. That's ownership.

Cage practiced for many days, both in the training bay and in the field until he could kill hundreds of Mimics without even looking. His senses and his movements became instinctive. He got better and better at the job. The result? He stayed alive longer. But one day he said to Rita, "We'll never get off this beach."

Cage connected with another Red Pill warrior, a bio physicist named Dr. Carter, from whom he learns that the armies of Earth have been fighting Mimics as individual soldiers when they are actually all part of a single organism: the Omega.

> "No matter what we do. No matter how carefully we plan, we can't get off this beach."
>
> ~Cage in *Edge of Tomorrow*[103]

Killing Mimics was pointless. Only taking out the Omega would win the war.

At this turning point in the movie, Cage realizes the beachfront battle is actually a distraction. To win the war against the aliens, Earth dwellers must shift their objective.

In our own ah-ha moment, we suddenly saw the difference between winning the battle of the Iron Triangle and winning the war against project failure. That moment rocked our world.

Trap of the Iron Triangle[32]

At the core of project management stands the Iron Triangle (a.k.a. the Triple Constraints of time, cost, and scope/quality). According to PM training, when a project manager can stay within those three lines, their projects cannot possibly defeat them.

Or can they?

If the Iron Triangle is actually bulletproof, why the 70% rate of project failure? Could it be that our best tool is also a factor for failure? In the world of project management, this idea is pure heresy.

Like shark hunters rely on the shark cage to protect themselves while meeting their "projects" face to face in the water, we rely on the Iron Triangle to protect ourselves from failure. In *Jaws*[33], as Hooper gets ready to take the shark fight into the water, he prepares the shark cage. Quint asks: "What d'ya have there, a portable shower or a monkey cage?"

When Hooper responds, "Anti-shark cage," Quint says: "Cage goes in the water, you go in the water. Shark's in the water."

As a marine biologist, Hooper had extensive training and figured he knew what he was doing. However, when the massive shark attacks his cage, we see how quickly his protection could become his deathtrap.

While the Iron Triangle can become a deathtrap in terms of defining project success, we also acknowledge that it can be helpful. Maybe we aren't using it right.

The Iron Triangle provides a framework for addressing the three fundamental project constraints with project managers and technical teams. It facilitates discussions when comparing strong, middle, and weak project constraints. Knowing which constraint is the softest in a project gives a place to go for relief when unforeseen problems come up. The strongest constraint is immovable and therefore slack is in the weaker ones. Simple.

However, the overwhelming evidence of failure says the Iron Triangle might be too simple. It cannot manage its own constraints or forecast outcomes in the practical world. Most project management experts recognize this. Several have tried to broaden the Triple Constraint Model into a diamond or star to bolster the Triangle's shortcomings.

The TRIJECT Model[34] incorporates and unifies Michael Dobson's theory of the Hierarchy of Constraints.[35] It's the best model we've seen, but something fundamental is still missing.

Michael Dobson is a good friend and coauthor of our last book, *Bare Knuckled Project Management: How to Succeed at Every Project.*[36] Michael is a prolific author, business consultant, and true project management master.

During an email discussion on March 14, 2016, Dobson said:

"Sometimes people confuse management's initial statement of the Triple Constraints ("Budget: $40m, Time: NLT 6 months, Scope: IT system upgrade") with the *real* triple constraints. A project is what it is, not necessarily what they tell you it is. We prefer not to spend more than $40m, but if the project will earn us $100m, it's worth continuing even if the cost doubles on us. If the upside is only $50m, then costs have to be kept under much tighter control."[37]

Dobson is in clear alignment with Kerzner. The constraints are what Operations Executives say they are. Unfortunately, too often these figures are not in full disclosure to the PMs on the front lines.

"Working within false parameters creates an equally false measure of success."

Here we come to the crux of the matter. Working within false parameters creates an equally false measure of success. Could a blue pill Operations Executive sometimes focus on protecting their own interests rather than performing at maximum effectiveness for the company?

Red pill executives are full-out committed to their project's success. They pull off the gloves and take the fight to the source. A Red Pill Operations Executive stops fighting Mimics and turns toward the Omega. A Red Pill Operations Executive kicks butt.

In his email, Dobson goes on,

I've never argued that triple constraints are the be-all and end-all of project management. They are a single tool and they provide a set of potentially useful insights, particularly useful in the very beginning when you're trying to understand all the hidden dynamics of the new project. The overlooked question, I argue, is "Why?" On the overall project, "Why are we doing this?" "What do we hope to achieve?"

"What will be different depending on whether we succeed or fail?" On individual constraints, "Why $40m? Why not $30m, or $50m? Is it a best-guess arbitrary number or is it anchored to a hard limit (the project's only worth $X, or we don't have more than $40m period)?"[38]

Michael Dobson is clearly onto something here. Project managers rely heavily on the Triple Constraints while their blue pill sponsors might have a different frame of reference and a different agenda.

Project managers often cite the "faster, better, cheaper: pick two" idea to their operations sponsor to set the stage for constraint discussions, but is it really that easy?

How can a project manager possibly make this claim without a deep understanding of scope, resources, capability, corporate culture, levels of performance, the temperament and direction of the Operations Executive, strategic direction of the company, and many other variables and considerations? If it were as simple as staying within the Iron Triangle, we would have a better track record.

In essence, project managers create presentations to deliver their analysis and estimates without knowing all the necessary background data. They need to know the scope of the work and the depth, breadth, and raw capabilities of the resources needed to handle that work. The seemingly intangible things like corporate culture really do matter and play a significant role in what resources are available and how they can be used.

"The blue pill model fails to recognize the far more critical and complex organizational context surrounding the project."

The traditional, blue pill model fails to recognize the far more critical and complex organizational context surrounding the project. The Red Pill Operations Executive acts in partnership with project managers. When everyone on the team pulls in the same direction, they get stuff done. Without this level of collaboration, the Iron Triangle locks the project manager into a doomed framework, sometimes to the point of taking the entire company down with the project.

While the blue pill Operations Executive hunkers down watching for Mimics hiding in the sand, their Red Pill counterparts assemble a squad of warriors and head out to kill the Omega, no matter what it takes.

Locking your operations manager into the Iron Triangle without regard for other factors leaves them exposed, where they can only move within rigid walls, where a shift in the cost, time, or scope/quality means certain death to their success, yet the project might need these changes in order to deliver Business Value. In situations like this, your operator is stuck between a rock and a hard place.

> "The battle is the great redeemer. The fiery crucible in which only true heroes are forged."
> ~**Master Sergeant Farell** in *Edge of Tomorrow*[104]

Long considered a place of safety, the Iron Triangle actually takes us down to where 70% of initiatives are eating our lunch.

The insidiousness of the Triple Constraint Theory is that we use it to judge our own performance. Hit pause and think about that for moment. The horrific success statistics we have been quoting are simply a record of whether or not we stayed inside the Iron Triangle. So much more is involved in evaluating project success, primarily whether the final result adds value to the company as expected.

Did you reach the company goal?

It's that simple.

Can you see the impact this bias toward failure has on PMOs within many organizations? It's no wonder PMOs are frequently formed and disbanded, reorganized and moved, while still confined to a structure and process that does not heal the damage to quality operations managers, the reputation of the Operations Executive, or the company's bottom line.

> "A true determination of project success is primarily whether the final result adds value to the company as expected."

This situation has become so dismal that many times the Operations Executive questions the effectiveness of project management altogether. After decades of disastrous results, agile practitioners completely reject project managers. The average Operations Executive accepts this rate of failure as par for the course for their PMO. They've given up on a lost cause.

Why? Because we've been working our butts off trying to kill more Mimics and dying on the beach while the real battle is far away.

Chapter 1 Summary

- The it's-just-the-way-things-are attitude is intolerable with failure rates at 70%.
- The industry has a deep inertia when it comes to improving effectiveness.
- Human behavior is at the root of project failure.
- Operations Executives and project managers who take ownership see improved performance rates.
- When used the traditional way, the Iron Triangle becomes a trap.

CHAPTER 2

What Does It Take to Win?

"There has to be a way we can win."

~**Nance in *Edge of Tomorrow*[39]**

In traditional project management, cost overruns, missed goals and deadlines, and even failed outcomes go with the territory. It's no wonder the average Operations Executive takes the attitude, *I'm already investing enough money, resources, and time on this. I'm not changing anything. Not even if it can increase my likelihood for success.*

Simply put, it's the devil they know, so they leave it alone. By the way, that's a perfect definition for blue pill thinking.

We've already established that project management statistics are attached to the Iron Triangle with a 70% fail rate. Lock yourself inside the Iron Triangle at your peril. While you're playing it safe, Jaws is circling and he's really, really hungry.

While we would agree that the Triple Constraints are vitally important, they are part of a larger pie. Every Operations Executive wants to keep

17

time and expense low and maintain the scope balance. That's how to get the most value.

However, when looking at overall project success, we have to widen beyond the Iron Triangle to Business Value and do that with a high level of clarity. No sugar coating here. No tweaked numbers to fit an agenda. No more murky statements like, "We're doing fairly well." Or "Nothing is wrong here. Especially near the nuclear reactor."

We're looking for *fidelity in the true value potential*. When assessing the Business Value of a project, think of yourself as a special ops sniper with a laser scope and a night sight. You're locking Business Value into the crosshairs, onboarding the squad, and heading straight for the Omega. This is where stuff gets real.

Measuring Business Value

How does a company accurately measure the Business Value of a project with *fidelity in the true value potential?* While the movie metaphor is a quick and easy way to paint the picture, real world project success is not as simple as blowing up the Omega. Business endeavors are complex, often with dozens of factors and many stakeholders.

Taking this question to the bare bones, we would have to say a win happens when the *benefit* of a project is more than the *cost*. This might seem oversimplified, yet without clarity on the cost and the benefit, the question of success or failure becomes so cloudy, the answer is impossible to identify.

You won't find the answer to the Business Value equation on a dashboard because some elements are subjective. Some elements are hanging in the air after a meeting's over. Some are in the movements of people in and around your organization. Despite the best intentions of those involved or the level of PMO maturity, the culture of your company and the biases of its constituents heavily influence whether an endeavor comes out as a win or a loss.

To get an accurate evaluation, the executive in charge must first find clarity as to whether the objective is worth the cost. When the Business

Value is high enough, sometimes it's okay to blow the time-cost-scope triangle on purpose. That's when the Iron Triangle becomes a constructive tool.

Sometimes, project failure can be an advantage. The highest order of business for an Operations Executive is to quickly kill a detrimental project before it funnels resources, time, money, and focus away from other activities that have more Business Value potential. Saving time and money before

> "Sometimes, project failure can be an advantage."

it's wasted constitutes a win for the organization. Sometimes this is a massive win, depending on how much time and money you are about to squander on something that makes no sense. Imagine how much money and time could be saved by canceling a medium-sized IT project, for instance.

When does an otherwise good project make no sense? When the Business Value doesn't merit the amount of time, money, and focus required to complete it. That comes down to Strategic Alignment. If the project is in Strategic Alignment with the purpose of the organization and its short- and long-term goals, then it is worth doing—as long as the Operations Executive has an accurate read on the Business Value potential.

If the project is not in Strategic Alignment, then it should be left on the white board. The same is true at any point during execution. If at any time the initiative veers out of Strategic Alignment, stop immediately. That's the back lot, bare knuckle approach we've been talking about. We know when to slam on the brakes, and we're not afraid to do it. We've saved our clients millions, and that's money already in the bank.

Measuring Strategic Alignment

To show how Strategic Alignment can be subjective at times, we thought back to a client we recently worked with on two significant initiatives. These projects were of such high importance that the board of directors of the company asked the president to take the lead as the executive sponsor.

Certainly, with the approval of the board and the president, the initiative was in Strategic Alignment and worth pursuing. Since it supported one of the highest priorities of the business, as stated by the board, it even warranted the cost for outsourced project consultants.

The team conducted its Rapid Control Process (explained in Chapter 6: The Currency of Effectiveness), created a plan, hardened that plan, documented risks, built risk mitigating steps into the plan, created a budget, snaked the documents to the constituents, and kicked off the work. Five weeks into the six-month project, the company dismantled the project, and the manager received new assignments. Those big objectives didn't happen.

Money went out, but not a single person was in trouble.

> "The company spends money to learn what doesn't work. We call it the school of hard knocks."

When we asked the firm's president, "Was this initiative a win or loss for the company?" his response was, "We learned a lot…"

The project as a whole dissolved, but some of the work continued in a modified way as part of regular operations. They all got a little smarter.

The stated strategic objective of the project didn't happen. The project landed in File 13, and the firm saved money. The only tangible win: learning.

Next time, the company will do things differently, not because the project failed, but because the approach failed. They learned that their approach could not accomplish their strategic mission.

This happens a lot.

The company spends money to learn what doesn't work. We call it the school of hard knocks.

Sometimes, it's necessary to spend money, time, effort, and focus to get more *fidelity in the true value potential*, but even then, we have no idea how the project will fare. This happens all the time in organizations all over the world.

In a story delivered yearly by a college professor, a young, newly minted department head hired an expensive consultant who promised to make the department more efficient, saving the company money. Unfortunately, the consultant failed. The investment was not recovered. The young department manager brought her printed resignation to her divisional vice president, confessing that she had lost the department a lot of money. The VP laughed and threw the document into the trash. "Resign?!?" he boomed. "How dare you offer to resign after we just invested so much to train you to make better decisions? Now get back to work."

> "Too often, the project succeeds, but it fails against the bigger mission of the business."

How do you measure a project's performance at this level? It's a business case. Sometimes it's an easy case to make – upgrading to a new CRM allowed us to track our customer preferences better, allowing the sales group to achieve their strategic goal of 20% growth and increase market share.

Other times, the business case is less compelling, murkier, or with negative outcomes – we learned a great deal, we won't make that mistake again, and it cost us less to learn than we otherwise could have spent. We'll take that as a win.

Failing in Strategic Alignment is the same way. If we opted for an unnecessary and expensive system upgrade as a growth measure when the business strategy was to invest in other, higher margin areas of the business, failure to remain in Strategic Alignment is clear. However, if we made that investment in system upgrades because our strategy was poorly constructed or terribly communicated, fidelity in the true value potential is absent, and people feel confused about whether it was a win or a loss.

Too often, the project succeeds, but it fails against the bigger mission of the business. To keep the project in Strategic Alignment, the Operations Executive and other relevant senior executives should attend project briefings to explore the true value potential and bring fidelity to the discussion.

That takes us into a company meeting, face to face with the most subjective and difficult factor to measure and manage: human behavior.

The Human Element

Once a project has enough merit to get off the white board, another factor rises to the surface: the human element. We come across the human element in every conversation, every interaction, every plan, and every meeting. It's about motivation and positioning. Sometimes we call it bias. Sometimes we call it perspective. Sometimes it's called WIIFM—What's In It For Me.

Strategy, tactics, and objectives are subject to "the humans"[40] and what they don't say out loud. Human bias impacts the measurement of project success at every level. Perhaps that's why the Triple Constraints became the standard. Measuring human perspective is hard to do.

Biases show up in different forms at different levels. Executive bias is different than departmental bias. For example, PMO leaders could be biased to measure process adherence. Project teams could be biased toward avoidance of backtracking.

A hypothetical project team might be biased to smooth operations. Supporting that bias, the corporate culture rewards predictability over speed. So, when the PMO measures the satisfaction of the team at the end of the project, the scores come back low because the team had to move uncomfortably fast. When the PMO weighs the opinion of the team members equally with Strategic Alignment, the entire report tilts off center.

Meantime, the hypothetical Operations Executive was motivated to move at maximum speed in this project because his promotion depends on a big visible project win, even though it means the added cost of ramping up more capability than really necessary.

The CEO accepts the win, even with the enormous cost and continuing overhead. His WIIFM includes a glowing report to the board. The strategic measures he shows them don't expose the unnecessary cost.

The outcome: skewed results that veer from the *fidelity in the true value potential.*

Bias complicates measurement.

Some would go so far as to suggest removing the human element as much as possible and using technology instead. They claim their model doesn't need people as project managers.

On December 15, 2015, Jim Johnson interviewed Ken Schwaber on CHAOS Tuesday podcast episode #103, "PM Agile Role."[41] Schwaber is the founder and president of Scrum.org and the co-author of *Software in 30-Days: How Agile Managers Beat the Odds, Delight Their Customers, And Leave Competitors in the Dust.* CHAOS Tuesday is a podcast production by the Standish Group.

During the podcast, Jim Johnson, chairman of the Standish Group, asked Schwaber the following question: "What role does the project manager play in an agile project?"

The following is an excerpt from that podcast:

> Schwaber: Jim, I usually come at that backwards. I back into it. And I say, well, there is the product owner and they're responsible for change management, and contingency planning, and making sure the product performs as it's supposed to and managing the risk in all those things. And communicating that the value is there for what's being built.
>
> There's the dev team and they're responsible for understanding the requirements and turning them into things that meet the definition of done and needs of the organization.
>
> There's the scrum master which is responsible for the smooth interaction of the team with each other for the creativity, for the productivity, for the team being focused on the work.
>
> So all the things relating to traditional software development like I just mentioned are covered by the three roles in scrum. Anything else, might be done by a project manager.

[Pause.] I'm not sure what that is, but I don't think it justifies the average salary of $130,000 a year...

He's not sure what else might be done by a project manager? Projects are bigger than the development effort. You have marketing, legal reviews, pilot efforts, cross-team communication, coordination, and the list goes on and on.

Back to the podcast:

Johnson: So, would the product owner who has project management skills be a good person to have?

Schwaber: Not necessarily. We think they deserve a fair shot at this, but usually they have habits of thinking their job is to tell the development team what to do rather than working with the development team to see what the best they can do is. So, I think they deserve a fair shot at that because they're part of the transition, but about 40% of them are able to make that transition in thinking."

Johnson: So, basically what you are telling me, if I hear you, and reflecting back, there is no role for traditional project management in agile projects.

Schwaber: That's right.

Johnson: ...PMI has created a whole agile section. They're even certifying people with agile project management skills.

Schwaber: They're trying to make it viable that you can say "I'm a project manager in an agile [environment], but that immediately has the project manager doing some of the product owner's work... So, it's talking out of both sides of your mouth.

Johnson: So, you would recommend anybody going to the agile community to take a hard look at the project manager community and the PMO and see if they're really adding value?

Schwaber: Yeah. They come from the right spot. They come from the right position. They're just used to executing it in a waterfall way. If you can help them get the insights, or they've just been waiting to execute the insights, they're perfect. But I wouldn't break your key on it.

Johnson: OK. I think you've disappointed a lot of project managers and PMO people.

Schwaber: "Well, they're good people, but it's time for change.

In software development, agile framework has taken the world by storm. Even the US Federal Government is adopting agile. There is good reason for it.

As Ken Schwaber clearly stated, there is no role for a project manager on an agile project. Everything is handled by the product owner, scrum master, and development team.

The product owner is an Operations Executive with product vision. They understand their business, are responsible for product features and capabilities, and work closely with scrum development teams to help with design decisions during each sprint. They are responsible for ROI, developing product roadmaps, and managing stakeholders. They create budget forecasts, track product performance, write user stories, attend scrum meetings, and are responsible for the execution of all tactical duties on the project.

This includes monitoring whether the project is going to roll out on time, on budget, and with the capabilities that were promised. Clearly, the creators of agile knew the Iron Triangle is a trap because they gave that responsibility to the product owner. If you're the Operations Executive in charge, the job of project management just fell squarely into your lap—folded into all your other responsibilities.

Looking deeper, does the agile model eliminate the human element? Not at all. They simply shuffled the deck, painted new pictures on the back of the cards, and called it a new game.

The human element is still very much in play.

Strategic Alignment and Executive Alignment

Whether using agile methodology or the more traditional Systems Development Life Cycle [SDLC], the waterfall model, the role of the Operations Executive is to carry out the strategy of the board and agreed mission of the company, both in the short term and the long term. Once the executive leaves the board meeting, influencers can make their execution imprecise, perhaps even misdirected or misguided.

Culture, ego, and relationships are the obvious influencers, but we knew there were more. In our research, we came across an article on TheBalance.com by Dan McCarthy, the Director of the Executive Development Program at Paul College of Business and Economics entitled, "The Common Traits of Successful Senior Executives."[42]

The Common Traits of Successful Senior Executives[43]

1. They are competitive.
2. They are dedicated to continuous improvement.
3. They work long hours but have come to terms with what "work-balance" means to them.
4. They know exactly where they want to go.
5. They love making decisions and can do so with limited information.
6. They expect solutions and hate whining.
7. They have "presence."
8. They are risk takers and don't mind making mistakes.
9. They manage by the numbers but don't lead by the numbers.
10. They regret not taking action on poor performers sooner.
11. They learn how to size up a team quickly.
12. They are rapid learners.

13. They multitask and tend to exhibit short attention spans.
14. They get bored with the status quo.
15. They have mentors and know how to leverage them.
16. They learn from experiences: good and bad.
17. They are strategic.
18. They have high expectations of others and readily show their frustration.
19. They manage up and play politics well in order to protect their autonomy.
20. They learn how to play well with their peers and build coalitions.

When we noticed that each element on the list could skew performance, we emailed Dan McCarthy and asked him how these traits could influence execution. He replied:

I think you've hit on some possible reasons. Others that come to mind are communication breakdowns (lack of shared understanding), lack of true consensus (silent disagreement), a dysfunctional executive team, the Abilene Paradox, power struggles, organizational structural and process issues that create misalignment or sub optimized execution, and a lack of top-level project management (like a structured monthly operating review (MOR).[44]

The Abilene Paradox

The paradox originates from the research of Dr. Jerry B. Harvey at George Washington University. Jerry tells the story of a dusty, hot afternoon playing dominoes with his family when his father-in-law said, "Let's go to Abilene and eat at the cafeteria."

The only available car had no air conditioning and no shock absorbers. With the temperature looming at 106° and 53 miles to drive in a dust storm over rough roads, the trip sounded anything but fun. The Abilene cafeteria had little appeal either. It was more like an Army mess hall than a restaurant.

Jerry's wife said, "Sounds like a great idea, but I don't want to go unless you want to go, Jerry."

Now Jerry had a dilemma. He didn't want to go, but he'd heard his wife say those words before, and it didn't go well for him when he refused.

So, he said, "Joy unbounded. I was just sitting here hoping someone would ask me to go to Abilene and eat at the cafeteria. But I don't want to go unless your Mama wants to go."

Mama said, "Of course I want to go."

They endured a grueling trip, ate a terrible meal at the cafeteria, and returned home four hours later.

When they got back to the living room, Jerry commented, "That was a great trip."

His father-in-law replied, "I didn't want to go to Abilene in the first place. I was just making conversation, and you idiots took me up on it! You ruined my day."[45]

Dr. Harvey's research showed him that the fundamental problem in contemporary organizations is not conflict, but rather the inability to cope with agreement. Most agreement in teams is actually false consensus. This occurs because many people expect to be ridiculed or censured if they voice objections. This often leads groups to act on inappropriate goals and sets them up for failure.[46]

Each item on Dan's list is driven by the mission of the business, but also influenced by culture, bias, and even the Abilene Paradox. Perhaps that is the difference between the most successful senior executives and those who struggle to find success.

This is the human element at the heart of performance. Every person involved has a sense of WIIFM tagging along on the ride to achieving the company's goals.

For example, Number 1 on Dan's list: "They are competitive." In large organizations competitive executives are an asset. This quality is key to achieving important corporate goals.[47]

But what happens in an organization without solid strategic development or executing tools? When an executive's WIIFM includes a need to compete, does that behavior influence Strategic Alignment? Absolutely. Poor strategic clarity, lack of accountability, overly political behaviors, and ego can lead to competition that redirects company activities away from its mission.

Humans like winning. However, what constitutes winning must line up with the mission of the business, or the project will shift out of alignment. This happens when a project has no Strategic Alignment but still has executive alignment. The executive sees the project as a potential personal win, regardless of where it falls within the company mission.

Let's look at Number 10 on Dan's list: "They regret not taking action on poor performers sooner."

What if the poor performer is a leader in the company or a project sponsor? What if that poor performer is a fellow executive?

Sometimes terminating employees is very difficult. Maybe the best that can be done is to move those individuals out of harm's way while strategic initiatives move forward. This twist in corporate culture also tugs Strategic Alignment off center... all the way to the top of the food chain.

A recent Gartner report entitled "Don't Leave the PPM Strategy to Chance" stated:

"But too many organizations leave strategy realization to chance. In a digital world, the probability of success due to chance is low, and the implications of failure are severe. This is why creating and executing on a solid innovation-driven strategy is key."

Gartner predicts that, by 2021, enterprises that commit dedicated organizational resources to ensuring that strategy is successfully executed will be 80% more likely to be industry leaders.[48]

> "As with many arenas in the 21st century, archaic blue pill thinking no longer wins the race."

If a company wants to rise to industry leadership, their success hinges on Strategic Alignment. As with many arenas in the 21st century, archaic blue-pill thinking no longer wins the race. We can no longer sleepwalk through life touting the party line and expect to rise to the top of the heap—personally, professionally, or as an organization.

The Gartner report further advocates creating a Strategy Realization Office (SRO). Quoting Donna Fitzgerald, Research Vice President at Gartner, the article goes on:

> Developing an enterprise-level competency for strategy execution, such as a strategy realization office (SRO) can provide significant competitive advantage," said Ms. Fitzgerald. "It not only increases the probability of success in the digital future, but also encourages the development of a cultural and human-centered competency rather than a technology or process-centered one.[49] [Emphasis ours]

People have more competency than technology when it comes to strategy execution. This is an interesting rebuttal to the idea that software programs and new methodologies are the wave of the future when, in fact, people are the problem.

The Gartner report goes on to say:

> Executing strategy is hard because the organization needs to begin thinking, investing, and ultimately, performing in the manner required by a new business model, while keeping its current business model operating to ensure short-term revenue.[50]

Bingo. Here we have the reason identifying and maintaining Strategic Alignment is so difficult in most companies.

> Finding, hiring, and retaining innovative employees to staff a construct like an SRO will be crucial if organizations are to succeed at executing new and evolving strategies. People who can deal with uncertainty, risk, and more-than-occasional failure will be required, making this a significant culture shift.[51]

Interesting that these qualities are key characteristics of high performing project managers. The article continues:

> For the foreseeable future however, strategy execution is the best all-around fitness program that an enterprise can adopt. Building the organizational muscle to run the race of effective strategy execution will be as important as winning the race.[52]

The Operations Executive controls how team members perceive the strategy behind a project. While the bigger mission of the organization might be clear, the strategy underpinning a specific project probably won't be. It's your job to chip away at your own preconditioning and squash your assumptions, your bias, and your WIIFM agendas. It's your job to maintain fidelity and lay everything out in plain sight. Then, bring your team into alignment as well.

"It's your job to maintain fidelity and lay everything out in plain sight."

Everyone who grows up on the Chesapeake Bay dreams of owning a boat. Jeff Welch, one of the coauthors of this book, was raised on the bay. A lot of his friends had boats, so when it was his good fortune to have the money to buy one, he called upon his network to help him locate the perfect vessel.

Two options revealed themselves: a well-kept fishing boat with a good-sized outboard motor and an aging 30-foot beast with two high-performance Chevy 350s. Jeff did not make the sensible choice. Dying to get his new boat in the water and satisfied that he had worked on it enough to make it sea worthy, he decided to go on a shake-down run.

In the protected creeks, that windy October day wasn't alarming in any way. But after leaving the sanctuary of the smaller creeks, he found that the bay was whipped into frothy three-foot chop. Jeff had been out in the bay a lot, but never in these conditions. He wouldn't have tried it in most boats that he'd been in, but this was a beast. His beast.

Without the proper level of risk mitigation or what we call spectrum analysis, he let'er rip and buried both throttles. That's when it happened. It was almost like a religious experience, an epiphany. At approximately 70 mph, the three-foot chop all but disappeared. The beast ignored them and plowed along like they didn't matter at all.

But then he noticed something else. Huge swells of water formed right in front his eyes. A lifetime of being on the bay, as well as many of the taverns around it, and no one told him these swells even existed. He watched them move and saw a way to mitigate risk.

Where they collided, the water surface lifted and became a mound he had to avoid. Where they parted, they left a giant hole, also best avoided. No one wants to drive into a hole at 70 mph.

So, there he was, witnessing a dance of swells that he had probably seen before but never knew existed. With this newfound perspective, he piloted the beast around the waist of the mounds, avoiding the holes, until he was satisfied that the beast was performing well and headed home.

It was a truly remarkable experience. The big takeaway: with the right change in perspective, you can see patterns that were just out of sight. Jeff didn't witness a new reality. Those swells had always been there. He was just lucky enough to be in the right place at the right time, so he could finally recognize them.

The problem with project failure rates has been around for a long time. People have tried to fix them for a long time, too. When we look around now, we see that almost everyone is focusing on the three-foot chop, thinking that if they eliminate those, they'll be able to manage their operations better. The truth is below the chop. It's those giant swells colliding and parting to change the project environment until continuing on your original course could prove disastrous.

The best way to avoid the swells is to maintain Strategic Alignment.

Choosing the Red Pill

Over the past few years, the entire project management industry has been struggling to figure out how to operationalize Strategic Alignment at the project level. Blue pill executives play their cards close to the chest, and blue pill project managers are not comfortable pushing boundaries. That disconnect in communication runs deep.

Enterprise PMOs are PMI's latest push toward Strategic Alignment, and this may be their greatest contribution to the space. Known in the industry as EPMOs, this task force monitors several teams at once, watching the overall impact of their projects on the company. Because they include top cover,

> "There's a difference between knowing the path and walking the path."[105]
>
> ~Morpheus in *The Matrix.*

EPMOs create a safe space, so it's easier to identify the swells beneath the surface and maneuver successfully around them.

Even agile methodology makes an attempt at forcing Strategic Alignment by handing ownership of the project to the Operations Executive. The executive already knows the Business Value potential and can act accordingly. That may be one way to do it, but piling extra duties on people who have no time or focus for them only creates other problems.

Strategic Alignment requires *fidelity in the true value potential.* This level of reality feels risky. Such a commitment to truth is very similar to choosing the red pill.

As Morpheus told Neo in *The Matrix*:

> You take the blue pill, the story ends and you wake up in your bed and you believe whatever you want to believe. You take the red pill, you stay in Wonderland and I show you how deep the rabbit hole goes. Remember, all I'm offering is the truth, nothing more.[53]

The Red Pill Operations Executive takes the risk and embraces transparency and clarity. This is where unvarnished reality is expected, discussion is open, and tough questions are welcome, even invited. Questions such as:

- If this venture actually costs twice the budget, is it still worth doing?
- How about if it takes twice as long or runs out an extra quarter?
- What if your corporate strategy changes and the goals of this initiative need to be realigned?
- What kind of reporting do you need to make sure you can properly communicate how this project stays in Strategic Alignment?
- Where is additional value that we can capture in and around this project?
- What are we overlooking?

When you have the *cojones* to work with team members at this level, you step out of the shadows and stand in the glaring spotlight. You also increase your personal capital and ramp up your chances to win.

Like we said, this is where stuff gets real.

You in?

Chapter 2 Summary

- As an operating model, the Iron Triangle must be demoted to a useful-tool status, replaced by Business Value with fidelity in the ability to see the true value potential.
- Saving major expenditures in time and money means a win for the organization. Quickly killing a wasteful project is also a success.
- Strategic Alignment is the best indicator of a project's ability to capture Business Value.
- A completed endeavor that fails to achieve Business Value isn't truly successful.
- Identifying real Business Value is sometimes complicated and murky, often intertwined with unsaid goals. Business Value becomes clear only by taking deliberate steps.
- Strategic Alignment is not the same as executive alignment.
- The Abilene Paradox, overly political behaviors, and other factors can skew perceptions of Strategic Alignment.
- Attempts to remove the human element from projects have fared no better than over-reliance on the Iron Triangle.
- According to Gartner, by 2021 enterprises that focus on executing Strategic Alignment will be 80 percent more likely to be industry leaders.

CHAPTER 3

Taking Off the Gloves

"Every champion was once a contender who refused to give up."

~Rocky Balboa

Chuck[54]

Starring Liev Schreiber, Elisabeth Moss and Ron Perlman

Millennium Films (2017)

Chuck is the true story behind the iconic movie, *Rocky*.[55] Chuck Wepner was a liquor salesman and family man with a modest prizefighting career in Bayonne, New Jersey. Suddenly, his entire life changed when Muhammed Ali chose him for a highly publicized title match pitting Ali against an unknown. Wepner went 15 rounds in the ring with Muhammad Ali in 1975 earning him the title "Bayonne Bleeder," the pride of Bayonne, New Jersey.

When Sylvester Stallone heard Wepner's story, he felt so inspired, he wrote the screenplay for *Rocky* and starred in it the following year.

We gave you the challenge, and you took it. You're in. You know your team needs to take the fight to the back lot and pull off the gloves. You know you can lead your team to operate on an upward trajectory for success during change initiatives known as projects.

We told you what we can deliver, and now we're going to get into it. Let's lock arms and march together through this process. We're going to build you a bare knuckled Red Pill team that kicks butt and takes names.

Remember the classic movie, *Rocky*?[56] Last year the movie *Chuck*[57] told the true story of Chuck Wepner, the man who inspired Sylvester Stallone to write *Rocky*. Both tell an inspiring account of an unknown who fights and wins against powerful forces.

However, neither Chuck Wepner nor Rocky Balboa are the focus of our study. Instead, consider trainer Al Braverman, known as Mickey in the *Rocky* movie. Braverman represents the seasoned mentor who has the street smarts to lead his trainee to victory despite all odds.

The Bravermans of this world aren't put off by a black eye or a bloody nose. They've stepped into the ring more times than they can count. They've taken the fight to the back lot, and they know the score. They have the street smarts to keep their trainee focused and grounded no matter what happens, whispering in their ear during the fight, cutting to the core of the issue in the midst of pain and chaos.

Braverman knew how to be the voice of reason when the fight had Wepner locked into survival mode. Braverman knew how to keep Wepner focused.

You are Braverman or Mickey if you prefer.

You have the *cojones* to stay the course when you reel under a sucker punch that would have the average person down for the count. You know what it takes, and you're determined to develop a team who can take it and keep on coming.

Most of the time you'll be coaching from the sidelines. You'll set the tone and keep things in perspective when someone on the team takes a right to the jaw. You'll create a no-BS environment where everyone has a voice and squashing a project that isn't working has as much merit as pushing through to the finish line.

"It won't be pleasant, but it's a problem we can fix. And you are in the right place to fix it."

You're ready to hold your team accountable to step up, own the process, and earn their place at the table, always reserving the right to walk away from a project that isn't working.

Pulp Fiction[58]
Starring John Travolta and Samuel L. Jackson
Miramax (1994)

Jules Winnfield (Samuel L. Jackson) and Vincent Vega (John Travolta) are hit men sent by gang-leader Marsellus Wallace to retrieve a valuable briefcase from a rival gang. After some gun play, Jules and Vincent obtain the briefcase. Shortly afterward, a hidden gang member bursts out of the bathroom and empties a large pistol point blank at them.

All the bullets miss Vincent and Jules. Jules is certain what occurred was divine intervention, but Vincent dismisses the idea. In the early morning hours, they leave with Marvin, Marsellus' inside man, in the rival gang. In the car, Jules continues his insistence that what happened in the apartment was a miracle. He says he's retiring from Marsellus' gang. Vincent leans back over the front seat to ask Marvin if he also believes in miracles and accidentally shoots Marvin in the head.

The inside of the car and both hit men are now covered in blood and brain matter. Furious at Vincent's stupidity, Jules drives to the house of his only friend in the Valley, a former colleague named Jimmie. Jimmie lets them hide the car in his garage but angrily tells them that they have to get rid of the body within an hour, before his wife comes home from work.

Jules calls Marsellus and wakes him up to explain their predicament. Marsellus then calls Winston Wolf, a suave and professional "cleaner." Wolf arrives at Jimmie's house and immediately takes charge. He tells Jules and Vincent to strip out of their business suits and get sprayed down with a garden hose. When they resist, Wolf tells them he's leaving and wishes them well. They quickly change their attitude and do what he says. He helps them dispose of the car and body at a junkyard.

Remember, Jaws is still circling. We all know it won't be pleasant fixing your shark problem. But it is a problem we can fix, and you are in the right place to fix it. We have the science and the tools. However, everyone knows the difference between a piano player who hits all the right notes and a true artist who deeply touches the listeners.

This is an art.

As with all art, everything begins with feelings.

In our example movie, *Pulp Fiction*, The Wolf is the project manager sent to clean up someone else's mess. Remember what that feels like? Remember that feeling in the pit of your stomach when you took on a new project, a sense that this is going to eat you alive unless you beat it and win? That prickly feeling is a vital tool. You might even call it the winning edge.

Using that uncomfortable feeling, you can start your team on the road to hacking their neurology. Relatively recent advances in neuroscience show that people have very specific cognitive limitations. In stressful circumstances, the human brain instantly shifts into survival mode. When a tree falls on the roof of the house, the homeowner stops balancing the budget and dashes for the nearest door or window.

> "Using that uncomfortable feeling, you can start your team to hacking their own neurology."

This fight-or-flight response helps people survive imminent danger. However, fight or flight works against you when managing complex projects because it interferes with your decision-making process. In your hurry to escape the roof collapsing, you could smash the $250,000 Ming vase that's your only inheritance and promise of a better future. In survival mode, you only know one thing: Get Away Now.

Your job as Braverman is to keep your operations apprentices in the flame longer. Use the fire to forge the steel. Help them become more focused and sharper than ever during times of stress.

You stand in their corner saying, "You're going to be OK." "Take a breath." "Try this…" You keep them focused as the punches keep coming.

This kind of training goes deep into the core of brain function to form responses at an almost instinctive level. This doesn't happen by rote learning, like memorizing the times tables. This kind of learning is infectious and transformative. It's based on specific thought practices, not systems or processes.

Changing the way a person thinks isn't natural. It takes motivation and follow through, but it is something you can build so deeply into yourself and your team that each of you instinctively knows what works. No more blind reacting and trying to pick up the pieces later. No more knee-jerk moments that sabotage your results—or at least a lot fewer of them.

When you cultivate teams of operators to act effectively in almost any situation, your company's management team or PMO will stay aligned with the *fidelity in the true value potential.*

In the chapters ahead, we're going to show you how to achieve high project success rates. We'll help you identify exceptional decision-making traits in team members, how to train your operators to think about projects differently, and how to put together teams that become an unstoppable force within your company.

No more dashing for the door. Now they stand and deliver.

Embrace Your Feelings

Project managers experience a wide spectrum of emotional responses that are tempered and influenced both by their training and their experience.

> "An operator who is not emotionally connected to their projects is only going through the motions."

A word of caution here, an operator who is not emotionally connected to their projects is only going through the motions. They have no ownership. Indifference will sabotage that person's results. No one can stay emotionally detached and properly manage a project.

Every operations manager should be able to describe how a new initiative feels in both gut feelings and emotional terms because every new project comes with risks:

- Personal risks: stress on the body, time away from the family, possibly sleepless nights. The project often becomes all-consuming.
- Career and professional risks: failure to meet goals, disappointing a client or supervisor, blind spots that can have a negative impact on the personnel folder.
- Risks to your reputation and the reputation of each team member. Colleagues will assess your worth not only by the outcome, but also by the way you handled the project.

Here's the bare knuckled truth. This job isn't for everyone. If you or your team member gets overwhelmed by a project, one of you might just make some excuse as to why you can't take it on in the first place. You'll feel that irresistible urge to get out now.

But what if you are the sheriff and a shark just showed up? People are dying on the beach. You can't afford an apathetic team member. You don't have time for someone who freezes or panics. That's why you don't assign Great White Shark initiatives to newly minted managers. Their fight-or-flight mechanism will paralyze them.

Like it or not, when faced with a shark attack you are a professional with a job to do. You assess the enormity of the problem and holler back to Captain Quint, in your best Sheriff Brody voice, "You're going to need a bigger boat!"

And, indeed, you are.

You need a lot more resources and bigger resources.

Your project is stopping Jaws, and one of you isn't coming out alive. Everyone in the boat scans the water—apprehensive but honest. They don't want information that makes them feel better. They want to know how big the shark is. As you write your project details on a company white board, a distant dorsal fin breaks the surface. Tension builds, waiting for the shark to get closer, so everyone can see it.

As it passes nearby, your project expert declares, "It's a twenty-footer!" but Quint, the grizzled old captain knowingly corrects, "No, twenty-five."

This is quite a moment. Your own experts can't agree on how big this project is. Like Sheriff Brody, you only really know two things: this is way more than you signed up for and even your veteran experts aren't sure how bad it's going to be. Your mouth gets dry. You have a lump in your throat, and your heart rate picks up. You suddenly yearn for a nice long walk in the park.

This moment is your training ground where you will transform average project managers into bare knuckled Red Pill operators. This is also how you will create Red Pill teams and, eventually, entire Red Pill companies.

A vital part of this process is getting clear on the role of each player involved. We call this the three-sided table (explained further later in this chapter). Each side of the table has its own perspective, its own responsibility, and its own markers for success. On the project management side of the table, the path to victory lies in the oldest parts of the human brain. Sometimes referred to as the lizard brain, this primal area generates responses like fight, flight, freeze, fidget, and a number of additional words beginning with *F*.

This moment is where you begin hacking the brain, so you can get the shark instead of the shark getting you. When done properly, your good project managers will become magnificent project managers. Big risky projects will happen routinely and successfully, and you'll develop a world-class operational team.

Own It

We call our own operators who exhibit this level of control Bare Knuckled Project Managers [BKPMs]. For the purposes of this book, we call them Red Pill PMs. Whatever their title, these highly trained professionals take ownership. Imagine how much easier your life would be if you had someone who takes a stand and gets stuff done. No more overwhelm. No more hovering. No more bracing yourself for the worst.

Like Marsellus Wallace in *Pulp Fiction*, when you get that call in the middle of the night, you will have someone you can depend on. You will have your own version of The Wolf.

Remember, you were once The Wolf yourself, poised and professional, ready for action. Then you became Braverman, training wolf pups to become kick-butt operators. When you developed your wolf pack, you became Marcellus, calling in your best Red Pill PMs to handle tough situations and trusting them to take care of business, as in our example from *Pulp Fiction*.

In the movie, Winston Wolf is at a party, complete with formalwear, when he gets the call. He takes some quick notes, realizes the gravity of the situation and immediately heads to the scene.

Problems don't happen at convenient times. Winston doesn't complain about how he was planning this party for months. He gets in his car and drives. That's what a member of your wolf pack does.

Rapid Immersion and Control

In our movie scenario, how much information does The Wolf have? Not much. He wanted to know who, what, when, and where. The Wolf didn't become a legend because he peppers his mind with questions or quickly jumps to conclusions. The Wolf engages in Rapid Immersion and Control. He jumps into his car and gets to the scene. He knows all the answers will be there.

He is totally dispassionate, even though the hitmen are in total freak-out mode.

He isn't concerned about relationships. He uses direct language, but he isn't rude. He doesn't come across as arrogant; he comes across as being in charge.

He is committed. He owns this problem for his boss, Marsellus. He climbs into the boat with the people he came to rescue. He puts his reputation as a fixer on the line. That's what the wolf pack does.

The Wolf arrives at the house at dawn. When homeowner Jimmie answers the door, he pauses at the sight of The Wolf's tuxedo.

Working from his notepad, The Wolf says, "You're uh, Jimmie, right? This is your house?" That pad shows Jimmie that The Wolf is in charge of this situation, no matter what Jimmie might have thought when he answered the door.

Jimmie needs to know someone is in charge, and that someone has an answer. Your team also needs to know who owns the situation.

When Jimmie acknowledges him, The Wolf says, "I'm Winston Wolf. I solve problems."

I solve problems. This is the best way to describe a Red Pill operator, what we call a Red Pill PM. Not all projects need rescuing, but once you have one that does, you need all the skills of a seasoned Red Pill PM on the job.

When The Wolf steps through the door, Jimmie suddenly becomes calm.

> "The Wolf didn't ask for ownership or test to see if anyone else would rather be in charge."

The Wolf is a totally buttoned-up kind of guy. Notice The Wolf doesn't ask for ownership or test to see if anyone else would rather be in charge. He takes control.

When Wolf sees the blood-spattered hit men, he politely says, "You're uh, Jules right?" Jules nods. "… and you must be Vincent?" Vincent also nods.

"Let's get down to brass tacks, gentlemen. If I was informed correctly, the clock is ticking. Is that right, Jimmie?" The Wolf identifies the critical constraint: time.

"You've got a corpse, in a car, minus a head, in the garage. Take me to it." He recites the facts. Accurately. Directly. Without emotion.

He makes a promise. He will fix things.

The team now knows three important things: The Wolf is in the boat with them. His reputation is on the line as a fixer, and he has command of the actual situation, not some rosy picture spun out by corporate.

> "Even under the strictest of time constraints, a Red Pill PM needs to demonstrate control and build trust."

Even under the strictest of time constraints, a Red Pill PM needs to demonstrate control and build trust.

Wolf asks direct and probing questions that make sense. This simple technique gives him enough initial control to hand out directives. He continues straight into Rapid Immersion.

Test for Risks

The four men move into the garage to view the gory mess. The team has seen it and freaked out already, so The Wolf pokes his head into the car window to see the mess, too.

With stunning calm, The Wolf casually says. "Jimmie, do me a favor, will ya? I thought I smelled coffee back there. Would you make me a cup?"

Jimmie asks him how he takes it. "Lots of cream. Lots of sugar."

As Jimmie hustles off, The Wolf continues, "About the car, is there anything I need to know? Does it stall? Does it smoke or make a lot of noise? Is there gas in it? Anything?"

Jules tells him the car is fine. The Wolf says, "Are you positive? Don't get me out there on the road, and I find out the brake lights don't work." Jules repeats the car is fine. At that point, The Wolf orders them back inside the house.

What was The Wolf's first reaction to the horrific sight? He asked for a cup of coffee.

A Red Pill PM manages desperate situations in a calm and deliberate way.

Control means everything. Once a member of your wolf pack accepts ownership, they immediately take full control and start to mitigate risks.

The Wolf saw Jimmie was of no use to the situation, so he sent Jimmie to make coffee. This established his authority and gave the man something useful to do other than stand around wringing his hands and questioning The Wolf's actions. Jimmie probably preferred the kitchen anyway, far from the car and its contents.

> "Control means everything."

When your team member is operating in the Red Pill bare knuckled zone, this maneuver is natural. It could be one of the first things one Red Pill PM recognizes in another. We call this ownership with rapid immersion and control. Without it, your team will face defeat before they get started. Without it, your project will end up in the 70% failure zone.

Example: Sending Jimmie for Coffee

A Red Pill PM is in a kickoff readiness meeting with a Chief Strategy Officer and their top lieutenant. In the middle of the discussion, the operator pauses for a second and says, "Hey, lieutenant, could you take just 10 minutes and build me a list of names of people working closely with this? I'll tell you why this is important later."

The lieutenant says, "Uh, sure. What details do you need?" The operator replies, "Name, email, and location." When the lieutenant complies, that operator thinks, *What do you know? I actually am operating in the Red Pill zone.* "Lots of cream. Lots of sugar."

Back to *Pulp Fiction*, The Wolf does a spectrum analysis and begins risk management. While he could simply deal with the situation presented to him, he takes time to consider what else could go wrong.

> "Red pill PMs slow down and wait beyond their first impulse."

Most people aren't good at this. Red pill PMs slow down and wait beyond their first impulse. Intuition can be a powerful tool, but it can also hide other options.

By pushing Jules and Vincent a second time, The Wolf made them consider possibilities they might have overlooked. When someone feels danger and uncertainty about a project, only specific training will help them stop and assess, not fire and forget.

It's significant that The Wolf ordered them back into the house. It again showed Jules and Vincent who was in charge. Second, it brought everyone back together, since further planning and tasking would require the entire team, even the guy making coffee.

> "This is the fine line between overbearing behavior and acting as a buttoned-up, consummate professional."

When they arrive, Jimmie gives The Wolf his coffee. He sips and nods.

That nod is exactly what a Red Pill PM would do—remain polite and gracious while exuding control. This is the fine line between overbearing behavior and acting as a buttoned-up, consummate professional. Appreciation for good performance is just as important as criticism.

Coffee in hand, The Wolf gently paces, his eyes sweeping the floor. Then he peppers them with directives:

"You two, take the body and stick it in the trunk." Jules and Vincent glare at him.

"Jimmie, do you have cleaning supplies?"

When Jimmie confirms, he tells the two hit men, "Clean the inside of the car. I'm talking fast, fast, fast. Now when it comes to upholstery, it doesn't need to be spic and span. You don't need to eat off it. Just give it a good once over."

> "The Wolf assesses the real task."

"Jimmie, I need blankets, I need comforters, I need quilts, I need bed spreads. The thicker the better, the darker the better. No whites, can't use 'em."

Turning back to Jules and Vincent, "We need to camouflage the interior of the car. We are going to line the front seat and the back seat and the floorboards with quilts and blankets. If a cop stops us and sticks his big snout in the car, the subterfuge won't last, but at a glance the car will appear to be normal."

Notice brains and blood in the car are not the real problem. If they had to make the car withstand close inspection, that would be a far bigger deal than what they had at hand.

The Wolf assesses the real task: they have to get the car and its contents to another location without being noticed. That's all they need for project success.

Focus Teams

Before he allows the team to break up and begin their assigned tasking, The Wolf paints a picture of his strategy, "camouflage the interior of the car," and places a quality standard around it, "at a glance the car will appear to be normal." Now they have a common vision to fill in any blanks they might encounter, so they can quickly move forward.

The Wolf spins toward Jimmie and says, "Jimmie, lead the way." Glancing back over his shoulder, he says, "Boys, get to work."

Vincent finally speaks up, "A please would be nice."

The Wolf stops in his tracks. "Come again?"

Vincent repeats, "I said, a please would be nice." This is a straight-up challenge to The Wolf's authority.

The Wolf deliberately walks back and says, "Get it straight, Bust I'm not here to say please. I'm here to tell you what to do. And if preservation is an instinct that you possess, you'd better flipping do it and do it quick. I'm here to help and if my help's not appreciated, lots of luck gentlemen."

Jules gets alarmed and speaks up, "No, no, no, Mr. Wolf. It ain't like that. Your help is definitely appreciated."

> "I'm here to help and if my help's not appreciated, lots of luck gentlemen."
>
> ~The Wolf, *Pulp Fiction*

Vincent cuts him off and continues, "Mr. Wolf, listen, I don't mean any disrespect, OK? I respect you. I just don't like people barking orders at me, that's all."

The Wolf quickly replies, "If I'm curt with you it's because time is a factor. I think fast, I talk fast, and I need you guys to act fast if you want to get out of this. So pretty please, with sugar on top of it, clean the --ing car." Without waiting for confirmation, he walks away and strengthens his position at the Three-Sided Table.

The Three-Sided Table

In our BKPM approach, we use the three-sided table to reframe the role of the project manager, even in agile.

Traditional project management has a two-sided table with the project manager and fulfillment team on one side, and the client on the other side. The project manager guides the fulfillment team and delivers results to the customer. That makes the project manager the advocate and architect of the solution. When the team succeeds, the operator succeeds. When the team fails, the operator fails.

On the other side of this table, the customer articulates what he or she wants. The customer applies pressure to the project manager to deliver the right solution at the right time and the right price.

In the BKPM method, we extract the project manager from the team and move the project manager away from a defensive position in this relationship. Here, the project manager doesn't represent either the fulfillment team or the sponsor. That frees the project manager to focus on the plan and the process of project execution, keeping it in line with overall business objectives.

At our three-sided table, every project has these seats:

1. The customer or sponsor who articulates a desired outcome.
   This is absolutely critical. If the executive sponsor cannot clearly articulate the desired project outcome in terms of *fidelity in the true value potential*, the project has little chance of success.

2. The project manager owns the process, not the outcome.
   Again, this is critical. The process is what enables consistent project success.

3. The fulfillment team delivers the outcome of the project.
   Under the direction of the project manager, this side of the table delivers the products or services. This side also represents the primary consumers of time and budget.

The three-sided table might use a traditional method such as Systems Development Life Cycle [SDLC], a.k.a. the waterfall model, or they might use agile methodology.

Sometimes the Operations Executive sits on the sponsor side of the table, but sometimes another person occupies that seat. This could be a department head or a client. Whoever that sponsor might be, they have a different perspective than that of the project manager and fulfillment team. The project manager might not be aware of how all the business's moving parts fit together. They don't know what they don't know. That's why you must never make the project manager or fulfillment team totally responsible for a project's outcome. The fidelity of sponsor communication affects the outcome in major ways, so it's best if the sponsor sits at the table to make sure those on the other sides of the table have got it right.

Once the others at the table have an accurate picture of the outcome, the sponsor doesn't need to micromanage the project. The project manager monitors the moving parts and keeps the project rolling toward success.

By using the three-sided table approach, everyone realizes important benefits, including:

The project manager observes and shares the findings. There are no secrets with the Red Pill PM. He or she is the honest broker to both the sponsor and fulfillment team.

The Red Pill PM holds everyone's feet to the fire. This means not only accountability but constantly moving the ball forward.

The Red Pill PM determines if risk is within acceptable boundaries.

The Red Pill PM challenges the proposed technical solutions and approaches.

The Red Pill PM has profit and loss (P&L) accountability for the project.

The Red Pill PM handles unnecessary escalations, so senior executives can sleep at night.

In our *Pulp Fiction* scenario, Marsellus is the Sponsor. The fulfillment team consists of Jules, Vincent, and Jimmie. The Wolf is the Red Pill bare knuckled project manager. If there were any question about this, The Wolf crushes it by saying, "Get it straight, Buster. I'm not here to say please. I'm here to tell you what to do."

This might sound a little too direct and harsh, but remember Vincent just challenged The Wolf's authority within the project. Even to The Wolf, this might have seemed a little harsh, so he tempered his response and took a little pressure out of the confrontation, "And if self-preservation is an instinct that you possess, you'd better --ing do it and do it quick. I'm here to help and if my help's not appreciated, lots of luck, gentlemen."

"The option for a Red Pill PM to stop an unworthy project represents the ultimate purity of the Three-Sided Table relationship."

The option for a Red Pill PM to stop an unworthy project represents the ultimate purity of the three-sided table relationship.

In our movie scenario, The Wolf's response to Vincent's challenge is pure genius. It's exactly the type of response a seasoned Red Pill

PM would have at the ready in this type of situation. Sometimes the Red Pill PM's only choice is to walk away.

Bottom line: if a project manager of Wolf's quality is providing value, no one will want them to leave a project. If, for whatever reason, the project manager is not providing value, he or she doesn't want to be there anyway. The Wolf was ready to walk away, not with malice or ill intent, but he didn't have time to waste time on coercion. If that's what it took, they were headed for failure anyway.

When Vincent agrees to comply, The Wolf is back in full control of the situation. He confirmed his dedication to the effort, and reinforced his position using a little humor. The humor aspect should not be overlooked. Power without a sense of humor and some humility doesn't work over the long haul. A highly operationally focused individual could sometimes demonstrate autocratic demeanor. However, when a Red Pill PM balances their strong leadership with a little humor and a smattering of humility, they become both directive and disarming.

A project manager who operates in a bullying style might be effective for a short while, but they will inevitably run into control and focus issues. The Wolf chose to explain his position and added a little humor to diffuse what was building up to be a bad situation.

It's important to recognize that The Wolf didn't have time to evaluate this situation, run through a set of possible outcomes, and then reach a formulaic conclusion. He didn't have time to recall that to achieve optimal team performance his communication should consist of 80% fact and 20% humor. His reaction was instinctive. It had evolved over countless interactions like this. After all, he's The Wolf.

> "His reaction was instinctive."

Given all of this, look at The Wolf's ending statement again: "If I'm curt with you it's because time is a factor. I think fast, I talk fast and I need you guys to act fast, if you want to get out of this. So pretty please, with sugar on top of it, clean the --ing car."

In this single statement, he went from being an aggressor to being a team player. He takes all of the pressure out of the situation with a single, somewhat ironic phrase.

This scenario has been an object lesson on the valuable role of a Red Pill PM in an emergency. This is what your wolf pack will be able to do once you've trained and empowered them for situations like this.

The Wolf represents your best Red Pill PM. As Braverman, you've trained your wolf pack to get the job done. When they are lined up, alert and waiting for your signal, you could be Marsellus—the one with lieutenants qualified and ready. Or maybe you are the one who delivers The Wolf to Marsellus.

Either way, what did Marsellus do when he got that phone call in the middle of the night? He speed-dialed The Wolf and spoke for less than a minute. Then he put down the phone, rolled over, and went to back to sleep.

That's what happens when you train a Red Pill team and let them own the project. Time and effort invested at the beginning reaps immense rewards in the end. It's the gift that keeps on giving—at the office, at home in the middle of the night, and even sipping Mai Tai's on the beach in Maui.

Chapter 3 Summary

- You're ready to hold your team accountable and earn their place at the table.
- Every new project brings an edgy feeling with specific cognitive limitations.
- Even in survival mode, you can train your brain to stand and deliver.
- Operators who are not emotionally connected to their projects have no ownership.
- With the right training, average project managers can become Red Pill operators who: own the problem, take rapid control, are 100% committed, mitigate risks, and reserve the right to walk away.
- The Three-Sided Table consists of:
  1. The customer or sponsor who articulates a desired outcome.
  2. The project manager owns the process, not the outcome.
  3. The fulfillment team delivers the outcome of the project.

CHAPTER 4

Finding Red Pill Recruits

"It was not a crash. We knew what we were doing.
It was a forced water landing."
~Captain Sullenberger in *Sully*[59]

Sully[60]
Starring Tom Hanks and Aaron Eckhart
Warner Bros. Pictures (2016)

On January 15, 2009, Captain Chesley "Sully" Sullenberger and his co-pilot, Jeff Skiles, complete a successful takeoff for US Airways Flight 1549 from LaGuardia Airport in New York City. Two minutes into the flight, a flock of geese fly into the jets, and both engines fail. The plane also loses radar.

Air traffic control urges Sully to return to LaGuardia. When Sully says it's not possible, they then direct him to land at Teterboro Airport just seven minutes away. Sully again responds that they won't make it. He continues to fly the plane and lines up with the Hudson River. He warns everyone on board to brace for impact, and seconds later the plane makes a smooth landing on the Hudson. Ferry boats quickly arrive and take people to safety. The entire process takes 24 minutes, and all 155 souls on board survive unharmed.

Sully and Skiles meet with the NTSB review board to examine the events of the forced landing. Although the actual engine hasn't been recovered yet, the investigators' report says the left engine was still functioning but idle. Sully insists he felt both engines die. Investigators then say their computerized flight simulators show Sully could have made it back to LaGuardia.

Sully argues that they did not take into account the "human factor." The test pilots were not under the same pressure that Sully and Skiles were facing, namely imminent death. These heroes not only faced the stress of a plane with no engines, but now they face the destruction of their careers as well.

However, more tests show that under the same circumstances, all test pilots would have crashed into the city if they had headed back to LaGuardia. Teterboro Airport was also out of range.

In the final meeting, Dr. Elizabeth Davis (Anna Gunn) comments that if Sully had been removed from the equation, everything would have gone wrong. Sully disagrees, saying that Skiles and the flight attendants also deserve credit for the landing. Davis asks Skiles what they would have done differently. Skiles replies that he would have done this in July. Everyone laughs.

Sully and Skiles ask for a break and retreat to the hall. When they are alone, Sully says to Skiles, "We did our job," and Skiles replies, "We did our job."

The best Red Pill PMs have specific traits that give them the ability to stay focused and continue forward progress no matter what's happening around them. Not everyone is cut out to work under such intense pressure. When interviewing candidates for our Bare Knuckled Project Management training, we might accept 2 out of 80 applicants.

The Red Pill operative is focused and disciplined, only slightly concerned with relationships, and less concerned with developing technical solutions. In *Pulp Fiction*, The Wolf didn't enter the house hoping to make friends. He also didn't pick up a sponge and go to work cleaning the car. He stayed on his side of the three-sided table and did what he did best: guide the project to success with simple, direct leadership what would get the job done.

The same is true of all our story examples in this volume:

The Wolf disposed of the car without attracting attention.

Chuck Wepner stayed on his feet.

Neo beat the Matrix at its own game.

Captain Sully landed the plane.

The primary task of any pilot in the air is to safely land. In 2009, when Sully found himself in a crisis with both engines gone, he stayed on task. His survival response was definitely online, but he didn't check out with an emotional meltdown. Instead, he kept interrogating the options while he continued to fly the plane.

Capt. Chesley Sullenberger had 35 years' experience in the air. He was the class "top flier" at the US Air Force Academy and earned his wings as a US Air Force pilot in 1975. He flew the F-4D Phantom II in the UK, then became a flight leader and training officer in Europe, the Pacific, and at Nellis Air Force Base. He was a Blue Force Mission Commander in Red Flag Exercises.

Sully had run thousands of missions in thousands of dangerous circumstances. When he said he couldn't make it back to LaGuardia, he couldn't make it back. When pressed for a reason why, Sully simply said, "I knew."

Interesting, that while in the Air Force, he was a member of an aircraft accident investigation board. Sully had not only experienced his own flights, he had helped investigate many others as well.

Sully didn't know how to communicate his reasons for choosing as he did because his responses had become instinctual. He just knew.

And he was right.

With training and experience over time, the bare knuckled Red Pill PM develops the same instincts. But how can you, the Operations Executive, know how to fill a team with people who can make the grade? Some applicants should never enter the program. Some wash out before their training is complete. Some go on to become the Wolf, and others become Marsellus Wallace.

While other factors, such as family problems, might interfere with a recruit's results, we've developed tools to make the sorting process easier and more efficient. As a result, our intake discussions look less like a typical job interview and more like special ops qualification.

Identifying promising red-pill-ready recruits is the first step to developing your Red Pill team.

How Personality Affects Recruit Success

Although successful Red Pill operatives have specific traits, these traits might be hard to spot at first because often these qualities lie beneath the surface.

"What distinguishes a promising Red Pill recruit is a way of doing business."

Sheriff Brody was a quiet family man. The Wolf had presence and flair. Neo was a tentative novice, Sully the confident professional. Major

Cage didn't know what was going on, and he sure as heck didn't want to get involved.

What distinguishes a promising Red Pill recruit isn't a particular personality style. It's a way of doing business. It's a combination of drive and how they relate to others. We have long used a set of four traits to understand the default or pre-developed traits of a recruit. These are:

- Operator – has a natural preference for completing tasks; if something makes their list, it will get done. They are great planners and are naturally detail oriented—but can get bogged down in the small stuff.
- Focuser – has a natural preference to lead teams. They drive others to commit to getting the job done no matter what obstacles stand in their way—but sometimes leave a swath of damage in their wake.
- Integrator – natural brain stormers and problem solvers with a never-ending supply of ideas—but don't always follow through and are notoriously bad at managing time.
- Relater – great at building personal relationships which often provides additional motivation for support—but can get so wrapped up in protecting relationships that they lose track of larger goals.

No single trait is the "right" trait. Each has advantages and disadvantages. Successful Red Pill PMs cultivate in instinctual preference to balance these four traits. Through self-awareness, hard work, intention, and maturity, each can limit their weaknesses and grow their capabilities to remain focused, direct, and effective in any situation.

> Develop a trusting affinity, so your protégé will stay in the fire with you when everything blows up.

When mentoring others, pay attention to their style. People tend to see their own style as the default, so if you move your own behavior toward matching theirs, you're more likely to get results.

Some call this building rapport or establishing connection. Whatever you call it, you'll need to develop a trusting affinity, so your protégé will stay in the fire with you and not head for the nearest exit when everything blows up.

Taking this one step further, we identified a way to see how these four traits work within the Red Pill model. We created a four-axis diamond made of Focuser, Operator, Integrator, and Relater work styles. The Red Pill PM archetype is inside the shaded area we call the Bare Knuckled Project Manager [BKPM] Resting Zone.

The BKPM Resting Zone leans toward the Operator with the other traits in lesser amounts. Operators tend to be detailed, accurate, organized, and methodical. The Wolf is an Operator.

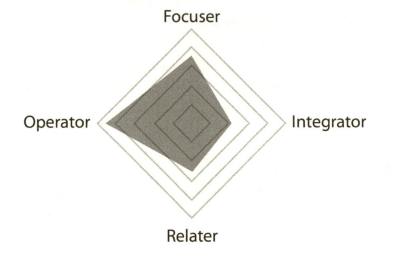

Red Pill Archetype

As the name implies, Operators are operationally focused. However, they could become so "operationally focused" that they are counterproductive. This type of Operator is obsessive, rigid, compulsive, and slow.

Moving clockwise, we find The Focuser, the second predominant type for a top-quality Red Pill PM. Focusers tend to oversee teams. Along with their natural leadership skills, they are determined, controlled, commanding, and authoritative. Again, there's The Wolf.

In fact, in a different situation, The Wolf might have pumped up to a more intense level of these traits. This is something anyone can do, but it's tricky to know when, and it takes energy. Focusers can also go too far and cross over into a counterproductive realm as well. When they do, they become domineering, autocratic, hard-headed, and tyrannical. You might recognize autocratic behavior in The Wolf, but he balanced it with humor and humility. Autocratic behavior is a detriment to long-term team performance.

The Integrator is weakest axis for the Red Pill PM, but that doesn't mean it's irrelevant. This type is more about maintaining areas of responsibility and accountability. Integrators are your architects, engineers, and innovators. They are imaginative, creative, energetic, and future-directed. While an asset at the right time and in the right place, sometimes a project manager simply needs to execute when an Integrator would like to hang out in the creative space. The Wolf was a bit of an innovator in the way he covered the inside

> "Operators and Focusers execute simple, direct and effective solutions that get results.

of the car. However, he didn't stay in the Integrator sector long. Once he crafted his plan, he swept into action without belaboring scenarios and looking for more possibilities.

Implementation is a Red Pill PM's reason for being, hence the strong leaning toward Operator and Focuser. They execute simple, direct, and effective solutions that get results. In other words, they get stuff done.

When PMs need an Integrator to solve a particular problem, they find one. This is why a Red Pill PM will often challenge the fulfillment team to come up with more than one development solution. Doing so causes the team to take another look at their assumptions and possibly find additional value.

Acting as an Operator and an Integrator at the same time is almost impossible. Integrators can be unrealistic, manic, unable to finish, and often lose track of time. You would not want these traits on your Red Pill team.

The final type is the Relator. Relators are team players. They are loyal, listeners, and sympathetic. Although admirable qualities, Relators can become a weight to Red Pill team because they easily slide into a conforming, reticent, and indecisive mode.

When the Relator trait becomes too strong, your PM will sacrifice productivity in favor of maintaining a relationship. They can become too sympathetic to drive the team forward and they will ignore operational details that would disrupt the cozy feel of workplace interactions.

The Wolf is empathetic but only to a point. He had some Relator traits, but his primary traits stayed in Operator and Focuser.

While not comprehensive, all Red Pill PMs have the above qualities. Please note: the objective is not to get as close to the center of the BKPM Resting Zone as possible. We are not creating clones. The BKPM Resting Zone contains a range of personalities that fit our criteria. Excellent project managers have work styles that fall within any part of the BKPM Resting Zone.

> Everyone outside the BKPM Resting Zone is not Red Pill material.

That being said, the BKPM Resting Zone has definite boundaries. All Red Pill PMs are inside that area on the chart. Everyone outside is not Red Pill material. Not that they are bad. They are simply not a good fit to be a Red Pill recruit.

Some people naturally fall within the BKPM Resting Zone. Others are close enough that, with a little development, they can hone themselves to exhibit those traits.

When screening your candidates, remember that many people can demonstrate these traits when things are going smoothly, but stress changes everything. If a candidate doesn't have blue-section traits as their natural tendencies, without training that person will revert to behavior that's in the white space when project goes haywire. Their performance will suffer as a result—70% of the time.

Before we sharpened our interview process to sort for Red Pill candidates, we conducted interviews like the average HR department. Screening, standard interview sequences, reference checks, lunch before making the offer—all the usual tactics. During that time, we interviewed a seasoned candidate whose resume looked fantastic. She was, without a doubt, a Red Pill natural. During our pre-hire lunch we pushed her with some really tough questions. She came through like the seasoned veteran she was.

We fell in love with our new superstar. She was that good.

We assigned her first client, one of our toughest. During the orientation process, she was tracking right along with us. We made the same promises we make to clients about Rapid Control and Fast Turnaround. When we turned to our new superstar, she crumpled into a meltdown under her first barrage of marching orders.

Looking deeper, we learned that under her amazing resume, her real-life skills were as deep as the paper they were written on. We had to let her go. Her resting zone was full out white. She had exerted significant energy to place herself in the BKPM Resting Zone on the graph, but stress moved her to her natural place in the white.

Sometime later, we created our scenario-based interview process. That's when Nancy Latusky appeared, a tall redhead, bubbly, and young with meager experience. In the scenario, we ratcheted up the stress. Soon, Nancy started flushing and sweating. She calmly asked if she could remove her jacket and carefully draped it over the back of her chair. Then, she stepped to the white board and took control of the project. We made her an offer, and she became one of the best we've ever worked with.

Stress is the great equalizer. Without it, you cannot tell for sure if you have a Red Pill recruit or not.

If you do come across someone whose natural tendencies are already inside the BKPM Resting Zone, half of the battle is already won. Strive to hire candidates with these traits whenever possible. However, even if someone is dead center of the BKPM Resting Zone, they still need training and they still might not make the grade.

Operating in the BKPM Resting Zone

Red pill PMs function inside the BKPM Resting Zone where the person is operationally disciplined, focused on the project management process and team progress, only slightly concerned with personal relationships, and not too concerned with creating technical solutions. Operating within the zone reinforces their position at the three-sided table and allows them to maintain an objective point of view.

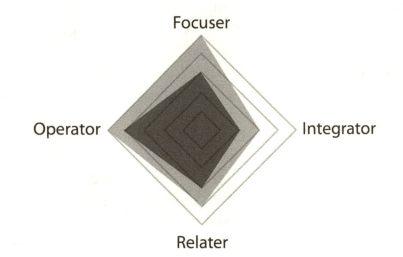

BKPM Resting Zone

In 2013, we developed an assessment to identify a candidate's project management workstyle position within our four-axis diamond. We call it our Resting Zone Survey. The Resting Zone Survey isn't an aptitude test. Instead, it indicates whether someone's natural instincts and preferences are consistent with the bare knuckled PM Resting Zone.

When someone's Resting Zone falls within the shaded area on the chart, that person is a natural. If they are within a certain range of that area, they can move inside with proper training. Using their assessment results, we help our candidates understand their management style and what it will take to become qualified.

The term, *Resting Zone* is significant. Anyone can use willpower energy to make it appear their workstyle is within the BKPM Resting Zone. However, during a crisis, that person will not have enough energy to stay inside the zone and will drift into the trait that provides the most personal safety.

> "Operating within the BKPM Resting Zone reinforces the position of the project manager at the three-sided table."

For example, when a project is running on time, on budget and delivering the desired results, anyone can manage it. If a project manager is lucky enough to have a project like this, it's a cakewalk. It's easy for that person to seem on point, doing all of the right things at all of the right times.

A bare knuckled Red Pill PM operates within the BKPM Resting Zone when the very worst is happening. If a project manager's natural tendencies aren't in alignment, remaining in the BKPM Resting Zone becomes impossible in a crisis.

> "A bare knuckled Red Pill PM operates within the BKPM Resting Zone when the very worst is happening."

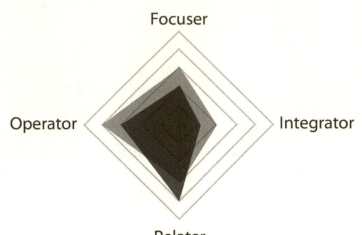

Focuser

Operator

Integrator

Relater

PM Zone While Under Stress

For example, let's imagine a project manager who loves to develop and maintain relationships. This person gets along well with everyone and may have completed a successful project or two. This project manager uses willpower to stay within the BKPM Resting Zone, even though most days end in exhaustion. As long as they have the energy reserves to keep it up, they assume everything is OK.

> "Combat is spontaneous and cannot be predicted but it can be controlled"
>
> ~from *Jeet Kune Do*

But what happens when the project goes completely off the rails? Where would this project manager focus when they run out of energy and cannot remain in the BKPM Resting Zone? In this example, relationships will probably take the day. Sympathy and soothing will take over when actually they should kick butt and take names.

However, even the best naturals might not make it through the program. People are subjective. Despite all the rules and guidelines, all the assessments and tools, some people will still stumble during the process. Human behavior is tricky. If this were easy, everyone would be doing it, right?

Think how many fighters Braverman trained and how many hit the sidewalk, never to return.

The Bravermans of this world know that as soon as a fight starts, conscious thought and planning are too slow. To win a fight on the back lot, every move needs to be instinctive.

Completing the training takes intense motivation. Hacking someone's neurology isn't pleasant. The Red Pill recruit has to endure stressors time and time again in order to develop *intentional instinct*. Some will become fatigued. Some will get angry. Some will throw in the towel before the first round is over. Humans want predictable, but this training focuses on the unpredictable.

Core Traits of the Natural

Working from the Braverman position, you need a strong understanding of the core traits that identify a Red Pill recruit. You want people like Chuck Wepner on your team: people who are unafraid of conflict. They work in a simple, direct, and effective style. Well disciplined, well trained, and versatile, they consistently move forward step by step until they reach their goal.

> "Victorious warriors win first and then go to war, while defeated warriors go to war first and then seek to win."[106]
>
> ~Sun Tzu

Unafraid of Conflict and Confrontation

If you're a professional fighter, you don't go around looking for people to beat up. Quite the contrary, in social situations, skilled fighters are often the gentlest, kindest people you will ever meet. However, inside the ring they go to work and get the job done.

When faced with trouble, these pros know the best tactic is to take fast action to untangle a complication before it gets out of hand. Confronting the problem directly and firmly means less effort and less conflict than ignoring it and trying to mop up after a FUBAR.

Of course, handling conflict can take many forms. Compromise and negotiation come first, but sometimes the project manager has to confront an issue firmly and directly with the idea that this will end here. Otherwise, they are not fulfilling their role.

This approach doesn't fall within the range of typical human behavior. Most people want to avoid conflict at almost any cost. They've learned that even winning a conflict probably means another bigger fight down the road. With training, the Red Pill PM recognizes conflict early and deals with it before it becomes a matter of someone winning or losing. In this way, problems get mutually resolved before a fight breaks out.

> "Results talk—bull walks."

Simple, Direct, and Effective

Unlike a kung-fu movie, pro fighters focus on the basics: simple, direct, and effective. Sure, they know the fancy moves, but they also know that 90% of the time the basics win the match. They practice a handful of straight, direct moves thousands of times until they become automatic.

An operations manager has dozens of fancy moves and cutting-edge tools like the Earned Value Method (EVM), the Program Evaluation and Review Technique (PERT), Monte Carlo simulations, critical path analysis, and network diagramming, along with a plethora of software.

Every one of these tools has its place, but most of the time they add complexity and don't get the job done faster or better. Simple, direct methods are usually the most effective. In other words, don't overcomplicate the process.

The Red Pill PM isn't tied to formalities. Results talk—bull walks. That's true no matter where the bull is coming from.

> "No matter how good you get you can always get better, and that's the exciting part."[107]
> ~Tiger Woods

Disciplined

On *The Matrix* movie screen, Keanu Reeves looked like he was moving spontaneously and effortlessly. However, Reeves had zero experience in martial arts of any form. He was an ice skater. Added to that, Reeves was recovering from neck surgery during pre-production.[61]

Despite his constraints, Reeves insisted on training and even requested training on days off. Only after five months of intense work did Neo's every move looked graceful and fluid.

Did Reeves get bruises during those 20 weeks of training? Did he get tired or lose his temper? Absolutely, but like his Red Pill counterparts in operations, he kept on until he got it right.

Teamwork matters, too. Trinity (Carrie-Anne Moss) and Agent Smith (Hugo Weaving) both sustained leg injuries during *Matrix* production. Smith required hip surgery. However, they finished the movie in good form. Self-mastery, concentration, practice,

> "There are no big problems, there are just a lot of little problems."[108]
> ~Henry Ford

and a commitment to excellence—those are the hallmarks of a disciplined team.

Over time, discipline and experience become art. But it doesn't stop there. The Red Pill operator keeps getting better and better.

Well-Trained and Versatile

Most Red Pill training takes place outside the classroom. Theory is no substitute for practical, on-the-job experience, so we emphasize practical learning.

Nobody—no matter how strong their natural skills, no matter how smart or capable—nobody becomes a *bona fide* Red Pill PM overnight. They start as team members, develop technical skills, and go through the lifecycle of projects. They experience the range

> "I don't look to jump over 7-foot bars: I look around for 1-foot bars that I can step over."[109]
> ~Warren Buffet

of surprises and problems that crop up. They become familiar with those that fail as well as those that succeed, and they pay attention to the reasons for both.

Red pill trainees learn to think in a simple, direct manner. They sift through the debris to find the real goal, and then focus on the best way to achieve that outcome. They identify what works and discard what doesn't. They stay flexible in their approach, knowing one size never fits all. They take care of business.

Moves Forward Consistently

As we know, the best defense is a good offense. First, you must approach the target to engage with it. Sometimes you speed up. Sometimes you slow down. Sometimes you expand. Sometimes you contract. But you always move forward.

> "If an operator can't take ownership of your initiatives, they are not qualified to become a Red Pill PM."

The commitment to forward movement is also a discipline. Most of the time the goal might be a bit muddy, but you can still make progress if you're generally moving in the right direction. Incremental improvement through continual progress eventually reaches the desired goal. One step at a time.

The Red Pill Attitude

During a recent seminar, an attendee asked us, "How do you encourage hesitant people to assume ownership?"

In public presentations and private training, we certainly inspire and instruct anyone in operations to take ownership. We tell them the value of taking ownership and talk about how to take ownership. However, we cannot make anyone take ownership. In fact, to be brutally honest, if you have an operator who can't take ownership of your initiatives, they are not a candidate to become a Red Pill PM.

> Captain Sullenberger: "My aircraft."
> Co-pilot Stiles: "Your aircraft."
> ~Sully[110]

Ownership is the Red Pill attitude toward any endeavor. Capt. Sully had two air traffic controllers instructing him to either turn back to

LaGuardia or go on to Teterboro. If he had given up ownership of his project, he would have crashed into New York City with a death toll that rivalled 9/11. Instead, he stayed in charge. He was the one holding the controls and sensing the movement of the aircraft. He was the one with 35 years' experience in doing this very thing.

Sully checked his options and went with his best choice. He saved thousands of lives that day—including his own life—because he took ownership.

> "A Red Pill PM always stays on the project management side of the table."

When a Red Pill PM takes ownership, the project feels like an extension of themselves mentally and emotionally. Whatever happens to that project happens to them personally. At least that's how it feels. When someone disrupts their process, or fails to perform or provide as promised, they feel like someone lifted $20 from their pocket. This shift in attitude transforms a flunky process manager into a bare knuckled Red Pill PM.

A Red Pill PM owns a project at a very personal level, but ownership does have its limits. Remember, in the bigger picture a Red Pill PM always stays on their own side of the three-sided table.

The Red Pill PM does not step across the table to own the business outcome of the project or the solution fulfillment. A Red Pill PM always stays on the project management side of the table.

As the project manager on duty, The Wolf wasn't concerned about whether or not the two hitmen were going to get off scot free. His project was ditching the car without getting caught. Once the car disappeared into the junkyard, The Wolf's job was done.

Fulfillment occupies a different side of the three-sided table. Project managers don't protect the fulfillment team, participate in solutioning, or decide when requirements are too vague. Not that the project manager gets to ignore such potential issues, they just can't own them.

> "If you want to train good operations managers, you have to empower them to take control."

Staying on their own side of the three-sided table allows the project manager to confirm that fulfillment has all the details covered. It is precisely this change in perspective that lets the project manager proactively address issues before they derail a project.

Ownership puts a whole new edge on change initiatives we call projects. A Red Pill PM would never allow a fulfillment team to endanger a project by not fully considering the thoroughness of requirements. That could blow the whole thing up.

A Red Pill PM would never allow an executive sponsor to change project scope without explaining in great detail all the impacts such a change could create. Nothing is ignored and nothing is absorbed without considering the impact on the project. The only way to be that passionate about managing the project is to completely own it.

If you want to train good operations managers, you have to empower them to take control. In *Pulp Fiction*, Marsellus didn't call every 10 minutes to check up on The Wolf. As the project sponsor, Marsellus knew the project was in good hands, so he let his Red Pill PM do his job. Marsellus also gave The Wolf the right to walk away if the project had no value. That's the purity of the three-sided table.

But what about when the worst thing that could ever happen suddenly happens? What about when your hair's on fire and the only liquid in the room is a bottle of Scotch? What then?

That's when you need a seasoned veteran, a Sully or a Wolf, on duty. No matter how good your natural recruits look, they still need training. The stakes are too high to throw a raw beginner into the mix and hope he figures it out. He might just crack open that Scotch, and you'll end up a scorch mark on the floor.

Eager novices are like Sully when he was back at the Air Force Academy, top of his class but still a fresh-faced kid with zero experience. No thinking person would have put young Sully in the pilot seat of a broken airliner going down over New York City. He simply wasn't ready.

That's where training and experience come in—where the brain's fight-or-flight response is on speaking terms with its analytical thinking. That's where you hack their brain chemistry and rewire it to meet the challenge. We call this limbic learning.

Chapter 4 Summary

- Not everyone is cut out to work under intense pressure.
- Operators and Focusers find simple, direct and, effective solutions that get results.
- Integrators and Relators are not as suited to managing team initiatives.
- Some people naturally fall within the BKPM Resting Zone. Others can hone themselves to exhibit those traits.
- Screen your candidates by adding stress and watching their responses.
- Operating in the BKPM Resting Zone reinforces the position at the three-sided table.
- During a crisis, only someone in the BKPM Resting Zone will not have enough energy to stay the course.
- The Red Pill recruit has to endure stressors time and time again in order to develop intentional instinct.
- Core Traits of the Natural:
  - Unafraid of Conflict and Confrontation
  - Simple, Direct, and Effective
  - Disciplined
  - Well-Trained and Versatile
  - Move Forward Consistently

CHAPTER 5

Rewiring the System

"Or, you take the red pill, you stay in Wonderland,
and I show you how far the rabbit hole goes."

~Morpheus[62]

For Operations Executives, the struggle is real. When working with people, you have to know when to push hard and when to take off the pressure. Knowing which tactic to use can be tricky, especially when one of these is surely out of your comfort zone. If you're Type A, pushing is your natural state, so relaxing actually takes more energy. No one can continually operate outside their comfort zone, what we call the *resting zone*, without strain. That applies to yourself, and it also applies to everyone working for you. But there is hope. Resting zones can be modified.

Over the years, we learned that asking anyone to use raw energy alone to operate outside of their resting zone is never a long-term fix and rarely even a short-term fix to any problem. We set up a framework that will show you how to understand your own resting zone. At the same time, you will see how you can hand out red pills to your team. Step by step, we're going to give you what you need to have them eagerly reaching for a glass of water and swallowing.

You're an executive, not a project manager, but there is no doubt that you still manage projects. You simply do it from an executive's perspective, so the first step is understanding where you stand within the project management archetype yourself.

In *The Matrix*, all Neo had to do was take the red pill and he experienced a complete unveiling of the differences between the false world inside *The Matrix* and true reality. The red pill was simply a metaphor for the paradox of choice. By taking a single red pill, he made the decision to open his eyes to reality. However, it's not that easy in real life. In sports, the arts, and in business, only a few superstars are naturals. The rest of us have to cultivate what we've got and grow into it.

The difference: energy. Without improving your resting zone, you're burning massive amounts of energy, forcing yourself to do things you dread. You arrive at the office with your shoulder forward and keep pushing until you leave the building.

If you are motivated, you and your team can improve your resting zone while staying within the parameters of good project management. You'll be in the sweet spot with plenty of energy to deal with stress. As a result, you will have a better experience on the job, at home, and in every area of your life.

> "When the worst happens, everyone wonders why the team leader didn't see it coming."

Some days are better than others. When the worst happens, everyone wonders why you, the team leader, didn't see it coming and all heck breaks loose. You know what I'm talking about.

Unless you and everyone on your team is a natural, the amount of energy you'll need to salvage FUBAR situations will stretch beyond your human capability. Like it or not, everyone will automatically revert to their default behavior and fail 70% of the time.

If a team member is relationship oriented, that person might struggle to make hard decisions affecting others. They could expend energy helping the delivery team find a creative solution and miss critical operational details. Their instincts will take them into habitual behaviors that might have worked in their past but aren't optimum in this situation. Unless their resting zone aligns with the project management archetype, no amount of energy will be enough to get them through when the bottom drops out.

For all of the power the brain gives us, it also has limitations. We call them blind spots. Magicians and con artists have capitalized on this for eons. It's neuroscience.

Even if a project isn't in full-blown meltdown, without this Red Pill shift in thinking, team members will miss dozens of cues signaling problems in the making because of blind spots. Everyone has them. Without training to recognize critical scenarios, you will certainly end up with your pants down and wondering what just happened.

> "Without training to recognize these key situations, you will certainly be caught with your pants down and wondering what just happened."

Here's how we phrase the choice of red pill or blue pill to our own trainees:

Do you want to believe you are truly in control of your own mind? If you do, and you like it that way, then take the blue pill, wake in your bed tomorrow, and go on managing operations the way you always have.

Or do you want to take the red pill? In that case, we'll show you some of the limitations of your mind and teach you how to hack it, so you can become better a better manager than you ever imagined.

Naturally, everyone wants to be better at their job, but most are skeptical and go into an "I'll play along for a while" response. That's when things get interesting.

The Neuroscience Behind It

Everyone assumes they're in control of their own mind, but exactly how much control do people really have? Teaching someone how their brain works makes them aware of what they are experiencing, so they can develop greater control over their behavior. Your bare knuckled Red Pill trainees are susceptible to the same pitfalls as everyone else, but with the right training, they will stay sharp and in control even in the middle of chaos and disaster.

The Hand Model of the Brain

Dr. Dan Siegel is on a mission to teach people how the two parts of the brain work together. To demonstrate the concept, he created the hand model as a simple way to visualize the various parts and their functions.

Hold your right hand in the air like you are ready to take a pledge. Imaging that your forearm is your spinal column.

Follow the spinal column up to the palm of your hand and imagine a circle that covers it. This is your brain stem. It's the very first part of the brain that evolved. This is where your primal instincts exist like fight, run, eat, and mate. This part of the brain is sometimes called the lizard brain.

Leaving your hand open, fold your thumb over the palm of your hand. The thumb represents the second part of the brain that evolved, sometimes called the dog brain. This is where emotions live like love, hate, loyalty, and distrust. The dog brain is also the source of all value-based decisions.

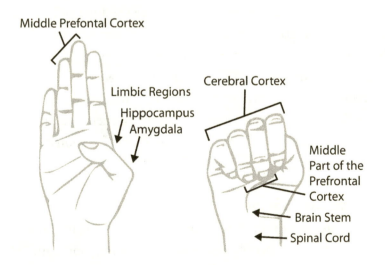

Hand Model of the Brain

This is a bit of oversimplification, but from the thumb down you have the dog brain, the lizard brain, and the spinal column. This is called the limbic system. Neuroscientists call it System 1.

Now take your fingers and fold them tightly around your thumb and bend your wrist down. There you have it. The hand model of the brain. This outer layer formed by your fingers represent the last part of the brain to develop. It is the new brain or neocortex, the part that makes us human. In the new brain, you find language skills, mathematics, information recall, and executive functions like analysis, planning, and prioritization. Neuroscientists refer to this as System 2.

Most traditional project management training relies completely on System 2—analysis, planning, and prioritizing. System 1 has no place in the curriculum. Doesn't it make sense that most project leaders go into limbic knee-jerk responses when the feces hits the fan? If the leader is a natural, all goes well. Unfortunately, most people are not naturals, so projects fail 70% of the time.

"Most traditional project management training relies completely on System 2."

Going back to the hand model of the brain, we see that emotions reside in the thumb, the dog brain of System 1, while language lives in System 2. Have you ever become so emotional (good or bad) that you couldn't find the words to express yourself? Everyone has. It's brain science.

Remember, value-based decisions form in the dog brain in System 1. This is where you decide if you trust your spouse, if the new intern creeps you out, or if you should you buy the chocolate bar at the grocery checkout display.

Much of our working model of the world lies within System 1, the limbic system. To change someone's behavior over the long term, you'll need to modify System 1. We call this limbic learning, and we will cover this topic in some detail later in the chapter.

"Much of our working model of the world lies within System 1."

Another brilliant neuroscientist, Dr. Daniel Kahneman won the 2002 Nobel Memorial Prize in Economic Sciences with his study of how the mind reacts to situations within the field of behavioral economics. Dr. Kahneman gives us a few more pieces of the puzzle:

System 1 – very fast, emotional, decision maker

System 2 – very lazy, logical, analytical, information recall

Systems 1 and 2 do not function at the same time, and often they lock each other out.

In Kahneman's book, *Thinking Fast and Slow*[63], he shares many examples to show how System 1 and System 2 interact. Here are a few of them:

Julie[64]

At age four, Julie could read fluently.

She recently graduated from college, and everyone is happy for her.

Can you guess her GPA?

An answer popped into your mind, didn't it?

Dr. Kahneman asked thousands of college students this question. The average answer was a 3.7 GPA. System 1 gave you that answer. It's lightning fast and it's intuitive. Did your guess match the research?

A Very Smart Man[65]

Let me tell you about a very smart man.

In fact, people say he is as tall as he is intelligent.

Imagine this man. Picture him standing in front of you. Can you see him?

Ok, so now here is the question—how tall is he?

Think about your answer. Did you say he was 8 feet or taller, or did you think nobody could be that smart? Did you say 5 feet or smaller, or did you think he couldn't be short because he's very smart?

System 1 took two completely unrelated facts, intelligence and height, and used your working model of the world to construct an answer. It happened without effort. It happened instantly, and it probably happened while lazy System 2 went on snoozing.

Most people feel very proud of their lightning fast System 1 and all of the power and speed that it provides. They should be. However, let's recall Dr. Kahneman's book title, *Thinking Fast and Slow*. In many endeavors, what makes us expertly human is the ability to slow down and interpret direction from System 1. That's why we obey laws and don't run around choking the daylights out of everyone who annoys us.

> "What makes us expertly human is the ability to slow down and interpret the direction from System 1."

Bat and Ball[66]

This example is fairly simple but important, so try hard to get this one right.

A bat and a ball cost a total of one dollar and ten cents.

The bat costs a dollar more than the ball.

How much does the ball cost?

In this example, Dr. Kahneman pits System 1 against System 2. Do you have your answer yet?

Most people allow System 1 to take this one, which comes up with the lightening quick answer of 10 cents. Good old lazy System 2 usually says, "Hey, if you want to take this one, go right ahead." But remember that System 1 isn't where our math skills are. It's where intuition resides—that gut feeling we act on in certain situations.

Lazy System 2 resists getting involved with the math usually fails to say the correct answer is five cents. The vast majority of people quickly decide the ball costs ten cents. However, adding $.05 to $1.05 gets you to $1.10. The bat is exactly $1.00 more that the cost of the ball.

While it's concerning that most people's System 1 pops up the wrong answer, it's even more concerning that System 2 didn't try to stop it. For some people, it's hard to override the quick answer even with additional information.

You might be thinking, "Good grief! Do I do this? Does everyone on my team do it? How many times does this happen every day?"

> "When System 1 pops up the wrong answer, System 2 doesn't try to stop it."

Taking this further, let's look again at Judy and her GPA. Did you choose a high GPA? If you did, your dog brain assumed that every question has to have an answer. However, in this case, the answer is barely a guess. You didn't have enough information.

What did you know? Judy was a fluent reader at age 4 and she graduated college.

Do you know what language she read and whether she went to college abroad where they spoke a different language? Do you know whether she was a party girl who never cracked a book or if she was highly motivated to learn? Did she have traumatic events in her life that affected her ability to focus?

Military intelligence uses a phrase called *shotgun analysis* where someone sees a set of data and makes an instant judgment with the speed and accuracy of firing a shotgun at a blurred and moving target. That is likely what happened with Judy's example. System 1 filled in the blanks despite incomplete data and came up with a quick response.

What about the Very Smart Man? He is as tall as he is smart, but that doesn't include any concrete terms. Although an answer comes to mind, no one can determine if it's right or not. Yet, people still feel certain about the answer.

These are good examples showing that System 1 is fast and System 2 is slow. If you don't slow down, System 1 will construct an unreliable answer while System 2 takes a nap. How many project rescue strategies and risk mitigation procedures have gone awry because of this one phenomenon?

Dr. Kahneman calls this WYSIATI [wiz-ee-ah-tee] or What You See Is All There Is. WYSIATI refers to a natural condition where we tend to not look for missing data. Dr. Kahneman says, "If we see a story, or some elements of a story, we construct the best story we can out of those elements and are really not fully aware of what we don't know."[67] He goes on to say that typically we also don't consider that the same story told a different way might produce a different answer.

> "WYSIATI refers to a natural condition where we tend to not look for what we do not see or recognize."

For example: which of these two steaks would you buy:
- One marked as 80% fat free.
- One marked as 20% fat.

As long as they're not vegan, most people would prefer to buy the package marked 80% fat free. It's the same piece of meat inside the package, but 80% fat free feels better. We don't slow down to think about a second description that is equally accurate.

Now we'll ask you the question we put to our trainees: "How often are you basing your operations decisions on what your gut tells you?"

This is the stuff project management horror stories are made of.

The Myth of Multitasking

In the modern world where people can be on three devices at the same time while monitoring kids and cooking dinner, most people would be surprised to learn that multitasking is a myth. It is only possible to multitask with two conditions in place:

1. At least one of the tasks is completely automatic, like walking and remembering an address
2. They involve different types of brain processing, such as reading and listening to music—but even then, your capacity is diminished.

What most people refer to as multitasking is fast serial tasking, shifting between multiple tasks in quick succession. And here's the kicker. While you are serial tasking, Systems 1 and 2 do not function at the same time. One can even lock the other out.

> "Multitasking is fast serial tasking."

While you are serial tasking, System 1 can be at the helm while System 2 is below decks. We've just seen how risky that can be when making good decisions. You can always pause to activate System 2, but you have to take time to do that. In a serial tasking situation, the mind becomes reluctant to pause.

What probably started as a survival mechanism can have undesirable effects in modern life. You don't need to analyze something large with big teeth that's running toward you. We're not fighting sabre tooth tigers any more, but System 1 still has major control as we cope with the pressures of career, family, and our complex society.

At times System 1 can become so engaged, that it simply will not release control to System 2. Someone in the throes of rage cannot assess the consequences of their actions. This is true of any extreme emotion, positive or negative, and also applies to the influence of alcohol.

On the other hand, when System 2 takes over, we can fall into analysis paralysis. System 2 sometimes gets so busy trying to compare, evaluate, and categorize that it will not release control to System 1 where value-based decisions happen.

Example: Analysis Paralysis

Imagine walking into a big box store to buy a TV. When you arrive, you see an entire wall covered with televisions. Suddenly you're face to face with the dozens of technical facts to consider. In your pocket you have a wish list handed you by your family.

Then the cost-benefit dynamic kicks in. You have to choose from 4K Ultra HD TVs, Smart TVs, Curved TVs, 3D TVs, LED TVs, Plasma TVs, and OLED TVs. What kind of surround sound should you get? What about pairing options? What's the energy efficiency?

On and on it goes. Soon a thick white fog mushrooms up, and you lose the ability to make a decision. That's when you need a trusted advisor to help you. Is it the opinion of the store clerk who works with these things every day? Or is it that a trusted friend just bought a TV like this? The value you put on their opinion can become the tie-breaker.

System 2 is powerful, but it can get so caught up that it will take over and not give System 1 the space to make a decision.

Example: Looking for an Exit, any Exit!

The phone rings. It's your supervisor, and he's mad as he gets. It turns out you missed a critical detail, and the whole project is now at risk. You know you should have spotted the problem before it got this far, but now it's too late. You already know what's going to happen next… and it isn't going to be pretty.

You are now System 1 dominant with your emotion engaged and your fight-or-flight impulses wide open. No amount of energy is going to get System 2 back in the game. For now, it's almost impossible to analyze the situation and formulate a recovery plan. You couldn't think your way out of a wet paper bag.

Without the proper training to embed better instincts within your System 1, you're done. Everyone around you might be clamoring for action, but your best bet is to take a walk, go out for coffee, or shoot some hoops until System 2 can come online again.

The Red Pill and Limbic Learning

We've beaten up your lizard brain pretty hard in this chapter. We've shown how it makes faulty split-second decisions when you should take time to do your homework before reaching a conclusion. Sure, System 1 has limitations, but it also has fantastic capabilities and holds the key to unlocking higher levels of performance. One of these capabilities is *neuroplasticity*, which lets the brain modify and adapt. Simply practicing new thought patterns over time will change the way you think and how you respond.

We've always known this about people. We constantly adapt to cultural changes, geographic changes, lifestyle changes, maturity changes, health changes, family changes, and on and on.

In emotionally charged situations, people can re-wire System 1 to slow down even in times of stress. We can also train System 2 to wake up and stay on the job. When done correctly, System 1 waits for input from System 2, then makes a sound decision. We call this *intentional instinct.*

When released together, the brain chemicals norepinephrine and dopamine open a window for increased neuroplasticity that lasts for 7 to 12 minutes. You can create this response in measured amounts by stimulating specific combinations of emotions:

1. Stress and safety
2. Novelty and uncertainty

Stress puts your mind in a heightened state (norepinephrine) and safety feels good (dopamine). Novelty feels good (dopamine) and uncertainty puts you into a heightened state (norepinephrine). This is a delicate balance. Too much stress or uncertainty and System 1 will have your trainees running for safety.

The brain doesn't distinguish between fake and real experiences, so role playing scenarios release the same dopamine-norepinephrine cocktail as on-the-job training. Bring up the right emotions in the right amounts and you can rebuild your neural network, what we call hacking your brain.

> "The brain doesn't distinguish between fake and real experiences."

Examples of limbic learning are all around us, but almost never in corporate settings. Some of the best examples are military Special Forces training, such as US Navy Seal training where they push their candidates to the brink and bring them back, creating the stress-safety dynamic.

This isn't about creating robots. Special Forces wants thinkers who can remain effective in situations that would fold most people into a fetal position. They want negotiators, team players, and shrewd warriors. This training is intense, expensive and, let's face it, not ever going to work in a corporate setting.

Let's take it down a notch to local police and firefighters. They also use stress and safety, novelty and uncertainty scenarios in their training. People in these professions train longer and harder than anyone would do in corporate life because they must react in ways that go against their System 1 programming for self-preservation. They run toward villains with guns. They run into burning buildings. They make quick decisions with lives in the balance, especially their own.

As a result, these trainees form new neural connections. Procedures become automatic, and their self-confidence grows.

A simple habit like touching walls with the back of the hand instead of the palm can mean the difference between life and death for a firefighter. If the back of the hand touches an exposed electric line, they will recoil and pull away instantly. If they follow their natural tendency and reach out palm forward, their fingers will convulsively grip the line, and they won't be able to let go. Imagine what it would take to make this simple move automatic while the ceiling overhead goes up in flames.

System 1 doesn't like the idea of burning to death, so without proper limbic learning, firefighters would get out of there and never go back.

Once your team begins this kind of limbic learning, their tolerance for stress and uncertainty will grow. They will see progress at faster and faster rates, like a bicycle picking up speed downhill.

Creating Lasting Change

Permanent behavior change has always been problematic. A study on adaptive leadership training published by the American Psychological Association addresses important elements for limbic learning.[68] The study showed that effective training must include two elements:

1. Experiential Variety—a stream of situations never seen before
2. Strategic Information Provisioning—a resource for tips and insights

Both new experiences and information must be present, or the behavior change won't happen.

Each experience must be unique enough to eliminate any default responses. Trainees must consider every situation from a variety of perspectives. This teaches them to question the first response from System 1 and push hard to discover all options.

For instance, their first response might be, "I'm scared." However, is that the best answer? What are they scared of? What are they scared by? Are they scared enough to run? Each perspective, or frame, delivers its own answer to these questions.

The moment you begin interrogating the first response of System 1, System 2 comes online.

> "The moment you begin interrogating the first response of System 1, System 2 comes online."

And here we are, back to thinking fast and slow.

When you twist the situation and look at it through multiple perspectives, this is called *cognitive frame switching*. This is a mind game, and it takes practice.

That's where coaching comes in. Coaching delivers the strategic information your trainees need so they can cycle through various perspectives and come to a strong decision. Without outside help, they will simply revert back to their usual behavior and see no change at all.

You might coach them before they begin the exercise, or you could deliver the information via a printed list for instant access in their moment of decision.

Teach them, "System 1 is not bad, but never trust it at face value. Interrogate your feelings." Then, make them tell you what they know.

With this method, both System 1 and System 2 learn to work together, and your success rates will rise.

Starting now, you can set up a limbic learning environment. Have your team members find a partner to act as their peer coach, then have them focus on identifying situations where:

1. They feel stressed—That's easy. It happens multiple times a day. Norepinephrine is never in short supply at the office.
2. They face brand new situations—Again, every day on the job.
3. Their coaching partner reminds them to see various perspectives and use new ways of thinking.
4. They find a viable solution.
5. They celebrate together while the dopamine flows.

With the proper planning and execution, every team member can feel like a Navy Seal candidate each time they arrive at work. Tens of thousands of Operations Executives and project managers face this kind of environment daily, but only a handful develop behaviors that increase their success.

Finding the right information, principles, and techniques to slow down System 1 and engage System 2 can be challenging. Follow through requires diligence and teamwork. This becomes even more difficult while in a busy work environment. The best results happen in a carefully controlled setting with trained coaches and proven systems.

Working with psychologists and veteran trainers, we wrote scenarios and included the strategic information to create a faster, more effective system. Our limbic learning framework uses sound Instructional Systems Design practices, but you can approach this is in many ways. It's not rocket science, but like anything else, it helps to build on top of the great work of others.

Our framework starts with our BKPM Boot Camp. Here's how it works:

After completing the Resting Zone Survey to identify where candidates appear within the quadrants of the bare knuckled project manager archetype, our boot camp candidates join us for about seven hours of live-fire scenarios. Consider it a fast and hard exposure to the bare knuckled Red Pill world. Through this process we show them their personality biases and show them how valuable their emotions can be when used correctly.

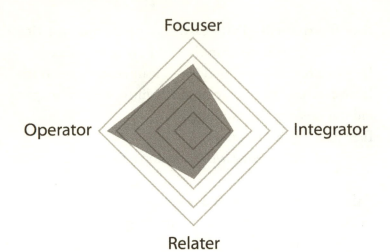

Red Pill Archetype

Afterward, we help them shore up their instinctual reactions so they can recognize new and better options in all situations.

We also show them how to access and leverage their feelings. That's right, their feelings. You'll not find this addressed in your typical project manager training, but we see that as wasted opportunity. System 1 uses feelings to track when everything is all right. When a person feels good and in control, everything is in balance.

An edgy emotion is the equivalent of a sports coach kicking a player in the pants to signal they're about to make a mistake. Paying attention to that kick is one of the hardest things to master.

Feelings flow in a constant stream, and most people learn to ignore them unless they get extreme. However, with awareness and practice, these emotions become little alarms that alert System 2 with a message: "Hey, System 1 is feeling off. You'd better slow things down a bit and see what's going on. We might need to look at the situation differently."

The moment they notice that edgy feeling, they should take time to investigate. They keep asking questions until they get to the truth, the whole truth, and nothing but the truth. This is where they will find better ways to take action.

Here's another example to pull it all together:

Example: Taking the Fight to the Back Lot

Let's say you're working on a project, and an email lands in your inbox. The instant you recognize the sender, you feel a little surge of emotion. Your morning is about to blow up.

You notice pressure in your chest and throat. You have an urge to get away from your desk. Your stress hormone norepinephrine is on the rise.

You tune in and become aware that you're feeling lack of control. Your first impulse is to ignore the email for about four hours and maybe it will go away. That's your fight-or-flight response, all reaction and no real action.

However, instead of taking a leisurely coffee break to get away from your email, you stop right then and interrogate the feeling. You think, *Maybe I should look at this from a new perspective and see if I can figure out why I feel this way.*

This brings back your control and that feels good. Whatever you are facing, you have managed to stop your blind reaction and set yourself on the path of intentional action. You get a tiny dose of dopamine.

This little process took only a few seconds, but it prepared your limbic system to start building new neural connections. You have 10 minutes to develop new instinctive responses to situations like this.

So, what do you do now?

You use your tools to interrogate your feelings and get back in the driver's seat where you belong. You have 10 minutes and counting to complete the process.

Stuck to the wall nearby is a list of bare knuckled principles. You scan it and hit upon Forced Conflict. You check in: *OK, System 1, does that help you see things differently?* System 1 responds with lightning speed, "Nope. Can't do anything with that."

Moving on…

You see the three-sided table principle and check in with System 1. This time you get, "Oh, am I doing that?" You realize you've somehow moved away from your position as project manager on three-sided table. You are operating from the perspective of the project fulfillment team.

You feel pressure because you are on the wrong side of the table. While your natural tendency toward empathy had some effect on your feelings, it's even more personal than that. Outside forces have been increasing and now the entire team, including you, is overcommitted.

The first thing you need to do is get back to your side of the three-sided table where you can look at things objectively. Then, you clearly see your need to revisit outside project demands with your project stakeholders.

Having a solid course of actions feels great and you get more dopamine. The edgy feeling disappears. You're back in balance and back on track.

Your 10 minutes has now elapsed. With repetition, you will no longer need to consult your printed list. Your instinctive reactions will be in the zone. Your personal success rates will rise and so will your personal capital in the department.

For training purposes, here's what happening in the above scenario from the neuroscience standpoint:

When the operator recognizes the email's sender, System 1 sends up its first response—a lump in the throat and an urge to escape. By pausing to interrogate the feeling, this operator is using *cognitive frame switching*. Exerting the power of choice feels good and releases a tiny dose of dopamine. These few seconds prepare the limbic system to start building new neural connections and the clock starts ticking. The 10-minute learning window is now open.

The printed list on the wall is *strategic information provisioning*. This trainee has the information readily available and can access it instantly. Scanning the list, the operator sorts and filters until hitting upon the best perspective: "I'm on the wrong side of the table, and my team is overcommitted."

First, the student corrected her own perspective. Second, she decided to revisit outside project demands with project stakeholders. Now she is headed in a productive direction. This is a much better solution than avoidance, the first response from System 1.

This isn't magic. It won't happen overnight. However, with motivation and the right training, limbic learning holds the key to unlocking this level of effectiveness.

When your team masters this concept, you'll have a squad of operations ninjas.

"By changing nothing, nothing changes."[111]

~**Tony Robbins**

Chapter 5 Summary

- Hack your brain to become aware of blind spots.
- Make a conscious choice to change perspectives, so you can fix your blind spots when decision making.
- The Operations Executive must take the red pill and convince team members to take it as well.
- The Operations Executive needs to understand their own Resting Zone as well as the Resting Zone of their team members.
- Understanding how the brain works makes way for change.
- Limbic Learning and neuroplasticity provide the framework for creating intentional instinct—the ability to make good decisions while under stress.
- Training for rewiring includes experiential variety, cognitive frame switching, and strategic information provisioning.

CHAPTER 6

The Currency of Effectiveness

Effectiveness is a rare and valuable currency in demand everywhere—from the boardroom to the classroom, whether you're hunting down killer sharks or landing a broken Airbus A320. Effectiveness gets stuff done in the real world.

In our movie example, *Edge of Tomorrow*, Major Cage's project was saving the world from alien invasion. To everyone, including the experts, that meant killing Mimics. He tried hundreds, if not thousands, of times practicing to get better and better at killing Mimics. Eventually, he could shoot without looking, reload, and shoot some more. He worked harder and smarter with every pass, but he wasn't effective. He kept losing. If he were a country, his Benjamins would have been worth less than toilet paper.

Effectiveness meant swooping in to kill the Omega and ending the carnage. It meant identifying the solution, activating resources, and winning the war.

If your definition of a project win is simply killing Mimics, your own dinars will slide toward the bottom of the Forex and keep dropping—no matter how hard you and your team work, no matter how many Mimics lie limp and lifeless on the sand.

Struggles with effectiveness often arrive disguised as other issues, such as:

- Time management woes that training and cutting-edge tools don't help much
- Project overwhelm—too many open simultaneously
- Office activity that feels chaotic with little actual advancement (a.k.a. "Look busy, the boss just walked in.")
- Too much Cost and not enough Benefit
- Company politics and personal agendas outshine real-world progress
- The constant search for a "silver bullet" to fix all of your problems

An effective Operations Executive and his lieutenant(s) can lead, facilitate, negotiate, navigate, and execute. They push like Al Braverman, and they hit like Rocky Balboa.

This willingness to push hard and do what it takes isn't always welcome in a corporate environment. Sometimes you end up with a fight on your hands. Can you and your lieutenant go six hours and fifteen minutes in the back lot, slugging it out for your most critical project?

Pushing hard isn't necessarily the same as being an unrelenting jerk. Any number of that kind of project sponsor and project manager can drive their projects right into the ground. Others consistently complete their deliverables at the cost of long-term team development. They're like the kid who makes breakfast for Mother's Day and leaves the kitchen a wreck. They serve up the meal but never end up as the family chef.

The right kind of effectiveness adds business value and while building operational teams that get stronger and stronger with each project. This is a specific skillset because projects are temporary and unique, and they are always about change. They force people to operate outside their comfort zones and form new ways of thinking.

Normal operations involve consistent activities that keep the lights on, including routine systems and processes, training and efficiency—a completely different approach from special projects. Whenever you try to push any part of an organization to move and change, inertia kicks in. It takes force—energy—to make change happen. Before long, people become uncomfortable. It's human nature. Conflict between project initiatives and standard operations is a fact of life.

That's where The Wolf comes in, a fighter with the energy to push the project out of inertia and into forward progress. The Wolf takes care of business, and he's tough enough to go the distance. Then at the end, he restores order to the organization and the feeling of *status quo* returns as a new normal.

A New Look at The Iron Triangle

A truly effective initiative acquires the most Business Value in the shortest time while expending the fewest possible resources. Don't misinterpret; sometimes, ample time and abundant resources are required to succeed. Acquiring the most Business Value requires first and foremost, succeeding.

When mentioning time and cost, we immediately think of the Iron Triangle, but the similarity is deceptive. At first glance, the variances might seem like small shifts in perspective when actually they are vital and non-negotiable differences. When you become strategically aligned and your goal becomes capturing the maximum Business Value possible, time, cost and scope must increase or decrease as the opportunity demands.

This is pure heresy in the minds of most project managers, but that assumes they have no idea what strategic alignment means. In our definition (simplified), a *project* is an opportunity to capture as much value as possible, through a set of coordinated and controlled activities. This change in focus from outcome to value lets us shine a floodlight on Business Value Potential rather than aim a flashlight at time, cost, and scope.

Project managers encounter hundreds of value-based decisions. These choices might seem insignificant to begin with, but they can have huge impact on Business Value Potential.

For example, let's say your project involves monitoring Quality Control [QC] on components. You have two options: use internal staff or outsource. The Iron Triangle sees this as a simple time-for-cost equation. Economizing on internal time resources might seem attractive if the outsourcing company submits a low bid. However, when outsourcing the job, you will lose insights about how to improve production quality. You could easily slide into the quicksand of outdated QC fixes.

Focusing on The Iron Triangle's rigidity could throw the company into a penny-wise-and-pound-foolish money drain that costs the business millions.

And your own effectiveness currency takes a nosedive on the Forex.

Such is the fate of many projects, taking quality project managers with them because shining a flashlight on the outcome leaves additional Business Value Potential in the dark.

In this case, the business value opportunity could be to develop a QC process that exposes the source of quality issues to the production team, so they can make practical improvements. Doing so might initially cost more and take longer, but the Business Value Potential might merit those expenditures.

> "When your organization sees an ocean of value, you want to cash in on the fullest measure of that ocean."

When your organization sees an ocean of value, you want to cash in on the fullest measure of that value. How many resources you will expend depends on the size of the ocean. Those amounts shift and change throughout the life of the project as your awareness shifts and changes. Remember, you will never capture all the value. It's impossible to cover the ocean.

Imagine the Iron Triangle floating in an ocean of value. The sides of the Iron Triangle expand and contract with the movement of the waves. The scope will change with discovery of more value, causing the constraints to change as well. This is effective project management with value-based goals.

With this larger context of the project in mind, you, the Operations Executive and sponsor, can bring that information to the three-sided table to improve the overall effectiveness of the operations team. When that happens, the project becomes opportunity-driven instead of simply completing an outcome on time, on budget, and within scope. Remember, those Triple Constraints rarely happen in the first place.

This shift in perspective produces several energizing results:

1. Instead of your project managers saying, "That's not my job," they adopt a strategic view of the project.
2. The technical team becomes evolutionary and finds ways to push their limits.
3. As you discover more Business Value Potential, the scope and constraints adapt as well.
4. You can now capitalize on marginal value opportunities.
5. The exchange rate on your own Benjamins goes up, so when you speak, people listen.

A New Perspective on Challenge

What if your project manager can help you clarify the *fidelity in the true value potential* by persistent use of the Socratic Method? How would that sit with you?

In *The Matrix*, Neo asked 94 questions, 56 percent of his lines in the movie. As the Red Pill PM on duty, he challenged his Operations Executive Morpheus at every turn, including:

Follow the white rabbit?

How did you do that?

How? What? Why?
What "Truth"?
Why do my eyes hurt?
What are you trying to tell me, that I can dodge bullets?
There is no spoon?[70]

As the Operations Executive, at times you might not be aware of the full strategic value potential. Maybe you have a blind spot in your perspective, or maybe you've been too busy to look up at the horizon. Invite your project managers to test, push, and question everything. Invite them to test all constraints to see where they fail, fall short, overestimate, or under-deliver, even to the point of testing your own perceptions by respectfully playing the devil's advocate in dialog with you.

Fearlessly question the Strategic Alignment of each project. Here are some examples:

- How does this project further our business strategy?
- As the Operations Executive sponsor, how does this project help you succeed?
- Where does this project rank among all your initiatives?
- How will other departments view the importance of this project?
- Do you still want us to proceed even if we can't show that it supports the mission of the business?

Afterward, task your project managers with communicating an increasingly clear value potential to the others at the three-sided table. Let everyone have a broader understanding of the Why behind the project and open the door for capturing even more potential value.

At the same time, whenever the perceived value becomes overstretched and unrealistic, scrap that idea before it costs the organization too much. Remember, killing an unworthy project is also a win.

When you grant your operators permission to challenge, you also unlock your own potential for greater effectiveness. Like the new Gatorade ad campaign says, "make your rival your fuel." It's the same kind of idea.

In our experience from years of working in the field, a project that's not on time or on budget is rarely considered a failure. The only failures are those that consume resources without capturing a corresponding level of value. When focusing on Business Value Potential, traditional measures for project success don't work.

> "When you grant your operators permission to challenge, you also unlock your own potential for greater effectiveness."

Red Pill PMs need a new system of measurement. We would like to see a system that measures the project manager's:

1. Awareness of the project's maximum value potential
2. Skill in leading a team to awareness of that value potential
3. The ability to capture the most value potential possible

Those who do well within this framework will be known as effective project managers who can stay in the ring with a heavyweight for 15 rounds, who can identify the Omega and take it out, and who can land the darn plane. Those who don't, or can't, will remained prisoners of the Iron Triangle and continue to fail 70% of the time.

> "Look, do you wanna play blind man? Go walk with the shepherd. But me, my eyes are wide ------- open."
>
> **~Jules Winnfield in**
> ***Pulp Fiction***[112]

Strategic Alignment: Business Purpose meets Project Mastery

In training Wolf cubs to become mature Wolves, you're leading them to mastery of control within each project. Whenever your Wolf cubs feel prickly vibes that things are spinning off center, they access their limbic system to regain control and predict the likely outcome. Complete mastery requires a broad range of skills and takes time. The more skills, the more your Wolf pack will progress in terms of type, breadth, size, and complexity of their projects.

You're developing a pack of project managers with training, experience, and self-mastery to run their initiatives like a mini-company. They have their gaze fixed on Strategic Alignment to your company mission, with their peripheral vision on the horizon to capture more and more value. They get the job done while minimizing risk as much as possible. This in contrast to traditional project manager who are blue-pill blind, their vision limited to project completion... and they've never even seen the horizon.

Management Statistics 2015 reports that only 18% of companies say that Strategic Alignment is how they determine project prioritizations. And equal number, 14%, report that either expected benefits or ROI are used. For the rest, more than 50%, no prioritization apparently exists.[71]

Your Wolf pack has two levels of strategy for their mini-company: project completion and business purpose. To meet both goals, they take entrepreneurial leadership and see each project

———————————
"They own it."
———————————

as an entrepreneurial endeavor. In other words, they own it.

To accomplish this larger vision, their approach and actions also expand. This might seem like more work—and in some ways it is—but it also allows more room to flex and move within their various roles. Turn them loose, and they will soon show you what they've got—for better or worse. We've said it before, and we'll keep on saying it. This is where stuff gets real. Anyone who can't take the heat ought to consider leaving the kitchen.

Case Study: MIRA:[72] An organization with a time management problem.

MIRA is a composite of several client companies. We have simplified their stories for example purposes. This hypothetical company has a project management organization [PMO] with seven full-time project managers, operating as advanced project coordinators. Very few of these project managers have the experience and skills to operate at the Tactical

PM level. They're too early in their careers. However, they are learning quickly, and this company provides great experience.

The PMO leader at MIRA has a traditional view of the role of the PMO.[73] She has the experience of a Tactical PM, but is not a Strategic PM or an Operations Executive. The Executive Vice President oversees the PMO and IT. He has high expectations and drives the team with deadlines—someone along the lines of Master Sergeant Farell in *Edge of Tomorrow*.

The team uses modified agile and has a beautiful, custom developed, robust Portfolio Management tool designed by their own IT department. Their program lists 148 active projects. Projects run a few weeks to almost a year in duration with most being several months long.

The Executive VP sees the team's performance as meager and on a downward slide toward dismal. Shaking up the PMO is one of his annual rituals.

Every single day, the project management team works frantically but never seems to catch up. Their personal time management is good considering the environment. They are forced to manage their time wisely or see immediate consequences from their hovering VP. However, any improvements in time management or processes don't improve the overall effectiveness of the PMO.

These are common problems among organizations struggling to create mature PMOs. The problems have everything to do with time management and yet getting better at time management doesn't fix the problem. Like Cage, they get better and better at killing Mimics but still can't get off the beach.

MIRA sent their entire team for Tony Robbins coaching, paid for efficiency training, and offered incentives. Despite all this company expenditure, their PMO could not work through their caseload of 22 projects per team member in a given year.

If the average project lasts four to six months, each person has about seven open projects at any given time. A full-time project manager at MIRA can spend less than five hours per week on any project in her active portfolio, due to non-project time she must also cover, such as meetings and scheduling.

Is the caseload too heavy? That's a band-aid answer. Let's look deeper.

From the perspective of these frantic project managers, they are constantly running through a forest where all they can see is trees. With such limited visibility, almost all trees start to look alike. They have no aerial perspective of the forest. They've never seen how they relate to the surrounding territory in MIRA land. There's no time for that.

> "It's not the daily increase, but the daily decrease. Hack away at the unessential."
>
> ~Bruce Lee[113]

Anybody with an instinct for self-preservation knows to invest the most time at the most important activities. They have no choice but to ignore the least important ones for the time being. The cause? Failed prioritization at a higher level.

Fixing this problem would not be easy.

MIRA leadership decided to address the problem head on. They started with a very simple question: Is everything listed in the Portfolio Management tool really a project?

That was a good first step. Here are some questions that helped them assess each one:

- What is the purpose of this initiative?
- How many technical hours and how much technical cost has the company invested?
- How many executive meetings have dealt with the scope, plan, and execution?

Digging deeper:

- Which ones have inadequate scoping and no real urgency?
- Which are fragments left from prior projects that should have been handed off during closing?
- Which have a fundamental break in initial assumptions on time, cost, and benefit, now hanging in limbo?

- Which are simply stalled?

Under the leadership of their Executive VP, with much effort and review, they cut the list until only 75 projects remained. This alone made the PMO look better—no more missed deadlines, better communication, and fewer mistakes. Now time management was more about improving performance.

But the process did not stop there. They divided the remaining 75 into these categories:

1. Top priority—where failing brings real consequences
2. From the top priority list—where applying the minimum effort will produce the maximum results
3. Those to ignore for now—they are on autopilot, slow, stalled, or abandoned

Finding Strategic Alignment

Asking that first fundamental question lead MIRA to a pivotal question: "Of the projects remaining, how many are truly important for achieving our company's current and future goals?"

That is the one truly important question. Are these initiatives strategically aligned with the business purpose now and in the future?

Here are signs that Strategic Alignment is on shaky ground:

- The objective takes dramatic shifts on a regular basis
- No one seems to care about the project besides the project manager
- The project manager has no time to run this project
- Other stakeholders have a low commitment to the project
- Dedicated resources aren't actually "dedicated"
- Resources to complete the project arrive slowly or not at all
- The budget is often pulled or reassigned

Bringing all initiatives into Strategic Alignment is one of the most difficult tasks operations leadership can take on. Gartner says, "Executing strategy is hard because the organization needs to begin thinking, investing and ultimately, performing in the manner required by a new business model, while keeping its current business model operating to ensure short-term revenue."[74]

This is the reason Strategic Alignment is so difficult. However, it can't be left to chance. It must be a competency of the executive team.

> Projects and programs that are aligned to an organization's strategy are completed successfully more often than projects that are misaligned (48% versus 71%). PMI's earlier research reported that aligning projects with strategic objectives has the greatest potential to add value to an organization. But on average, organizations report that three of five projects are not aligned to strategy.[75]

Doing a good job on fewer important things is better than doing a poor job at everything possible. Focusing on what matters—isn't that what effectiveness means? With Strategic Alignment, the operator can finally see the forest instead of dashing headlong, dodging trees.

Attaining Strategic Alignment requires executive participation and leadership. The operator needs the discrimination and discernment of the Operations Executive sponsor to know what is strategic and what is not. This level of performance makes small improvements highly impactful.

Companies that master Strategic Alignment succeed. Gartner further reported that "… by 2021, enterprises that commit dedicated organizational resources to ensuring that strategy is successfully executed will be 80% more likely to be industry leaders."[76] That is a great incentive!

"Build Strategic Alignment into your project initiation process."

In order to effect change at this level, the key is to build Strategic Alignment into your project initiation process. Include Strategic Alignment in planning and make veering off course a risk you talk about often. Confirm it in project meetings in front of stakeholders and others at the three-sided table. Celebrate at the project's close where you can demonstrate how much you respect *the fidelity in the true value potential* made possible by consistent Strategic Alignment.

In their journey toward Strategic Alignment, MIRA cut their projects further until only those that aligned to the businesses purpose and mission remained. With intention and effort, they built a clear case for each project's alignment with the strategic vision and needs of each sponsor.

Here are their steps:

1. Inventory all projects
2. Bucket each project by the strategic goal it serves
3. Analyze the results:
   - What happens to projects that don't fall into any bucket?
   - If 70% of all project costs are directed toward only one goal, is that a problem?
   - Can these projects be further prioritized?

MIRA was committed to positive change.

Strategic Alignment requires full commitment to using projects strategically. This might seem like semantics, but it's a fact. Lip service won't fill the bill. Pet projects might go into File 13. Projects whose only merit is the elevated position of their founder might end up at the bottom of the list. These are hard facts with real-world emotions tied to them.

To maintain Strategic Alignment, every project launch must include a charter and the rationale proving the project is strategically aligned. The various business groups of a company must buy into the value component and cooperate in focusing on strategic projects.

> "Strategic Alignment requires full commitment to using projects strategically."

In the end, MIRA had only 53 remaining projects. These were vital and required considerable focus. With fewer projects and a stronger connection to the mission and purpose of the business, the project managers felt more welcomed and appreciated. Morale went up, and so did their effectiveness. Their PMO's currency was also on the rise.

At MIRA, the PMO team and Executive VP added strategic vetting to the scoping and approval for all new projects. Project sponsors would need to argue for and justify the rationale for their projects within the context of larger business purpose, every single time.

The PMO team felt substantial impact on time management. Here are some of the noticeable improvements that followed this shift:

- Forced focus on projects with the greatest impact
- Aligned projects to executive focus and sponsor outcomes
- Allowed each operator to prioritize project activities for maximum effectiveness
- Focused technical team efforts
- Created opportunities for continuous executive engagement
- Resulted in better time management and efficiency all around
- Allowed the Operations Executive to fully create his vision through the operator
- Built Strategic Alignment competency for both the operator and the Operations Executive sponsor
- Pushed Strategic Alignment down through the organization

At the end of the day, MIRA saw a significant increase in its PMO performance. Once unshackled, the team's time management challenges scaled back, and they were able to get on with their work.

Taking Effectiveness to the Next Level: Scalability

With Strategic Alignment as the center of your project universe and effectiveness clearly within your sights, roles within the team become more defined. Not all project managers are created equal. Some are more creative and others are more analytical. Some grasp the bigger picture and others line out the steps to get there. Both are vital to success.

Along with strategy, a complex project also needs someone to manage operations. These are two distinct functions. In our Red Pill model, we call these two roles the Strategic Project Manager and the Tactical Project Manager.

Like any executive, the Strategic PM views the project from a multifunctional perspective: operations, sales and marketing, finance, human resources, procurement, and the rest, as well monitoring Strategic Alignment. The broader their frame of reference, the more effective the Strategic PM tends to be. Former executives often make great Strategic PMs, although this isn't universally true. Entrepreneurs tend to do well, too, although they are often less structured.

The operational part of the project belongs to the Tactical PM. The key is balance between the strategic and the tactical, properly addressing the needs of each of these roles, and making sure time is spent on both perspectives. Most project managers spent their time tactically focused.

If one person fills both roles, the Tactical PM must intentionally schedule time to wear the hat of the Strategic PM and switch perspectives. This is not an easy task, and the industry doesn't train for it. We call this *role shifting*, and we train our team to do it effectively. You can, too.

In our BKPM practice, we us a simple, direct, and effective *Rapid Control Process* which incorporates both the Strategic and Tactical roles into the structure of the project from the outset. Using the Rapid Control Process, we swoop in to take control while simultaneously focusing on the strategic and the tactical elements.

Rapid Control Process

Strategic PMs are veterans who have served many years as Tactical PMs. They present a clear vision of the project's end game with both Strategic Alignment and project strategy in mind. They lead Discovery and Immersion meetings where the team explores the ocean of value and the Business Value Potential within that ocean. Then they develop criteria for a win. No more Mimic body counts. They want nothing less than the Omega.

With their success criteria in hand, they break the steps down into objectives that will drive the project forward. They come out with a strategic plan that ticks off the boxes and also makes sense for capturing value. That's when the Strategic PM comes to the three-sided table to share these initial thoughts with the project sponsors.

Here's where the sponsor's feedback and pushback are vital. Here's where free sharing of company mission and purpose lay the foundation for Strategic Alignment. Here's where the project gets its first pass or fail for effectiveness.

True, the project could get derailed later, but without this solid foundation, the project is often doomed before it leaves the whiteboard. While the effort might go to completion, the Business Value Potential becomes a lucky bonus with blindfolded operators playing pin the tail on the Omega.

Together, Strategic and Tactical create the Straw Man, the early draft project plans. They validate the plans, mitigate risks, and achieve active control of the project. The starting bell dings and it's Game On. Tactical quickly moves to the center of the ring and takes control of the project.

Tactical PMs are quick learners who are driven, astute, nimble, highly detailed, and analytical. They partner with their Strategic PM to mitigate risk and manage the three-sided table. They sit in the driver's seat of project operations. While they might integrate into an existing client team, they remain highly tactical and operate at arm's length. Like The Wolf, they aren't too concerned with relationships and are more concerned about getting the job done.

While Strategic PMs are on the front lines in discovery meetings with key stakeholders, their Tactical partners turn that information into solid, comprehensive project plans. Going forward, the Tactical PM manages the project schedule, weekly meetings, and weekly status reports. This is a true partnership between the two roles with clear delineation between the roles.

Although one person sometimes operates in both functions, the better approach capitalizes on the thinking of two distinct people to make plans less fragile in response to risk. It's rare that two people with two different approaches and two different histories will have all the same blind spots. Indeed, two heads are better than one.

Along with limbic learning, other types of thinking come into play with successful project management. At times, your project managers will need to be *effectual reasoners* who use seat-of-the-pants adaptation to deal with contingencies in the moment. At other times, they will need *causal reasoning* which is methodical and structured.[77] Both of these are highly operationally focused to continue moving the project forward. For our purposes, we specify these as two modes: Strategic and Tactical.

Most Operations Executives want all of that in one person. Needless to say, they are often disappointed. Executives use systematic causal thinking, but they need someone who thinks on their feet, who can manage the ups and downs of daily events. The truth is, stuff happens. One email or one phone call can blow everything up. The person at the three-sided table who handles those situations is the Tactical PM.

Operations Executives and project managers who work in some range of effectual to causal reasoning usually aren't equipped to be operationally focused, the same way a play director has someone else as the stage manager. Any project needs all these roles covered. In bigger, more complex initiatives, these are usually best served by different people working to the best of their natural talents.

This role division happens in all approaches, whether waterfall or agile. Agile developers argue that the person responsible for all of these roles is the Product Owner: you the Operations Executive or sponsor. We don't have to tell you that delivering all of this consistently day in and day out is a stretch, whether in an agile environment or not. What individual can switch back and forth between effectual, causal, and operationally focused reasoning well enough to address the Strategic Alignment, project strategy, and tactical elements of each and every project? It's just not realistic.

This is like asking Sully to act as air traffic control, fly the plane as it descended to the Hudson, and prepare the passengers for an emergency landing, all at the same time.

This complexity makes the demands of project management overwhelming for the vast majority of project managers. Despite their best efforts, putting in long days with project details swirling in their heads 24/7, they continue chasing a carrot that remains out of reach.

However, assigning these two distinct roles to the appropriate people will quickly give upward mobility to your success rates. When this happens—and it surely will—you'll have some people asking for your secret sauce. Some will want in on the action, and news of the Red Pill outbreak will spread. Depending on your corporate culture, you'll have to pucker or duck because something is going to hit you right in the kisser.

Chapter 6 Summary

- Struggles with effectiveness often arrive disguised as other issues.
- The right kind of effectiveness adds business value and while building operational teams.
- Normal operations take a completely different approach from special initiatives.
- To capture the maximum Business Value, time, cost, and scope must flex as opportunity demands.
- When you see an ocean of value, cash in on the fullest measure of that value.
- Clarify the *fidelity in the true value potential* by persistent use of the Socratic Method.
- Fearlessly question the Strategic Alignment of each project.
- Grant your operators permission to challenge you and unlock your potential for greater effectiveness.
- Companies that master Strategic Alignment succeed.
- Strategic Alignment requires full commitment to using projects strategically.
- Scale your effectiveness by using both Strategic and Tactical managers on your team.

CHAPTER 7

Spreading the Red Pill Mindset

"You will get all you want in life,
if you help enough other people get what they want."
~Zig Ziglar[78]

Corporate change happens at about the speed of tort reform. So, how does a single Operations Executive disseminate the red pill to others until a blue pill organization buys into the Red Pill perspective?

Typically, it's an organic process. First, someone catches a vision for something more and better. They choose to swallow the red pill and their success rate rises above the norm. Others notice and begin sending work to this Red Pill operator because they get things done. The Red Pill operator hands out red pills, and a few others in the company take them.

Soon, an informal Red Pill task force forms. Word gets out about their effectiveness, so more and more work flows in their direction. Over time, the company's blue pill PMO might collapse as they have less and less work sent their way. Eventually, the informal group could become a new Red Pill PMO.

This process has dozens of iterations. Many companies continue using *ad hoc* teams and never formalize a Red Pill PMO. Some formalize it and spread the Red Pill philosophy throughout the organization.

Sometimes the C-Suite catches wind of a Red Pill movement and shuts it down. Certain types of company cultures can't tolerate a Red Pill mindset. When a shutdown happens, the Red Pill operator has a rich supply of Effectiveness Benjamins and the confidence to find a better position within a Red Pill-friendly organization. That's the beauty of this model.

Although many variations happen, we've identified four stages in the Red Pill evolution.

Stage 1: The Red Pill Operative Becomes a Sage

The blue pill mindset assumes that maturity automatically means greater effectiveness. Conventional wisdom says, "Practice makes perfect." Yet, professional performers know the truth is, "Practice only makes permanent." If someone practices a flawed

> "What you practice matters."

technique, when they face a challenge, they will lose 70% of the time. What you practice matters.

However, taking the red pill is only the beginning of the journey.

Neo went through Red Pill University with courses in Red Pill perspective, limbic learning, and front-line experience. Morpheus knocked him down again and again and dared him to get back up. Neo had his share of black eyes and split lips, but he saw these as part of his development. He had a reason to get up and keep slugging until he became a ninja in a black leather coat. He built up his effectiveness currency until his team followed him, and they saved the world.

On a slightly different tack, in *Edge of Tomorrow*, Cage started out a victim of circumstance. He tried to play by blue pill rules, but he soon learned that he would never win that way. Rather than go down in defeat, he took control of his situation. He learned what it meant to be a Red Pill warrior. He went to battle and felt the pain of defeat hundreds of times. Cage continued his limbic learning and front-line experience until he transcended his mentor, and eventually Rita had to catch up.

"Cage freely offered his wisdom to all takers."

Rita made Cage pay for her mentorship with her edgy condescension goading him on. Cage did not take on her attitude. He freely offered his wisdom to all takers. He had nothing to prove. He was comfortable with who he was: a sage, an old warrior, a seasoned veteran who had the good fortune to lose his physical scars in the resets while his internal scars remained deeply embedded. He needed those internal scars to keep him grounded and make him wise.

"A Sage's quiet success attracts attention."

He became so calm and comfortable with who he was that he had no attachment to recognition or even promotion in the army. He could easily move on whenever he wanted. His effectiveness currency would speak for itself.

A Sage's quiet success attracts attention until others gravitate to them to learn their secret. Success is a master teacher.

This deep, internal calm flows from the soul of the Sage. This is not a fake-it-till-you-make-it environment. Rocky couldn't fake it in the ring. He had to take the beating. The Red Pill perspective is just as visceral as going 15 rounds with a champion. If you're trying to fake it, you'll end up back at your default position outside the BKPM Resting Zone. Only this time you'll have egg on your face and your credibility account will be bankrupt. It happens every time.

"These posers end up destroying the Red Pill system they are trying to build."

Worse, these posers will end up destroying the Red Pill system they are trying to build.

Case Study: Mardia, A Company Who Thought the Red Pill Was a Great Idea

Some time ago, an Operations Executive at Mardia saw effectiveness as a good working model and presented it to the C-Suite. They all agreed it would be a helpful addition to their internal PMO, so they bought a lot of our BKPM Pocket Guides[79] and handed them out to everyone in the company.

They got excited and even created an internal training program. They taught their project managers all the tricks in the BKPM Pocket Guide and set them to work.

However, what they didn't realize was the impact their company culture would have on the Red Pill model. Just a few days into the transition, they started facing tough decisions:

- Should Project A take priority over Project B, or not?
- How effective is this familiar tactic we've been using since Day 1?
- Should an executive pet project get shut down?

Whenever they had to choose between their culture and the Red Pill perspective, they chose their culture. In effect, they decided the following components weren't important:

1. Strategic Alignment
2. Business Value
3. Limbic Learning
4. Etc., etc., etc.

It didn't take long before they destroyed their Red Pill PMO—which was actually a blue pill PMO wearing a red jumpsuit. They failed to see the Red Pill system must come from core belief in order for it to work.

"The Red Pill system must come from core belief in order for it to work."

Years later, new leadership came into the company. They saw what was happening and said, "The Emperor has no clothes. Your PMO isn't effective." The organization had to start over from Square 1 and work on company culture first.

In our experience, the core question about whether the Red Pill model will work in a given environment always comes back to company culture.

If executives don't have the same definition for effectiveness, if the culture is highly political, if the focus is overly sales driven, cultural blind spots will undermine the Red Pill PMO. When difficult situations arise—and they always do—leadership will make a tradeoff and sacrifice effectiveness.

As we recognized this trend, we began to ask, "Can a Red Pill Operations Executive be effective in a company's current culture?" The answer: not always.

> "Can a Red Pill Operations Executive be effective in a company's current culture?"

If the culture rewards silos, accepts turf wars, and upholds protectionism, those distorted behaviors will take priority over effectiveness every time. In this case, the Red Pill Operations Executive will have to make incremental passes at improvements and spread effectiveness slowly. Otherwise, the Red Pill model will break.

Rarely does an executive hold enough personal capital that they'd risk expending it all in order to correct a busted culture. As soon as their leadership sees them as a heretic, the Red Pill operative will have to fight every step of the way. This type of fight requires strategy and stamina, and at the end of the day a win might not be worth the cost. Sometimes the only win is a move to a new organization.

Case Study: A Company Wanting Red Pill Results While Keeping Their Blue Pill Mindset

Some years ago, an Operations Executive in Wisconsin contacted our offices looking for help. They had an internal PMO that couldn't meet their deadlines. When they did meet their deadlines, the results were less than optimal. Expensive software, additional training, hiring seasoned project managers—none of these seemed to help. They lost project managers at an astonishing rate. Everyone in their PMO stayed stressed out and overworked. They just couldn't keep up.

In our first interviews, we discovered a high turnover in employees was causing problems in their HR department. They had customer service headaches, and a disgruntled engineering department that was difficult to work with.

We'd seen this kind of situation many times and felt confident we could help. After a few phone calls, they flew our team to Wisconsin to conduct an assessment of their situation and give them a recommendation for how to take positive action and increase effectiveness.

We arrived and went to work. A few days later, we handed in our report. The next morning, we sat in an opulent office with the Operations Executive and the head of their internal PMO to discuss our recommendations.

What we had found was an over-emphasis on sales. This company valued sales to the point that they sold products before they were finalized, sold more volume than the delivery team could handle, sold ideas before they had been developed, and sold and sold and sold.

This put immense pressure on their engineers who could not de-bug the software fast enough to meet their deadlines. Because their products arrived to the customer late and often with flaws, their customer service phones stayed lit up.

Those at the top drove new cars and ate five-star lunches every day. Those at the bottom could only withstand the pressure for a short while before they bailed. HR struggled to handle the volume of new hires. Customer service had a constant barrage of problem calls and mostly new hires to handle them. The Engineering Department stood under a firehose of demands, and they were mad as heck.

This company's culture saw Business Value as one thing: sales.

From our Red Pill vantage point, effectiveness meant bringing the various components of their business into balance, including customer service, customer retention, product development, product creation, marketing, and sales. We made an assumption that this company was setting up for the long haul. However, that's not what effectiveness meant to those in leadership. For them, effectiveness meant more sales. Period.

They didn't care about customer retention. They didn't care about bringing balance to the company for longevity. Their executives saw the PMO's primary goal as keeping the discontentment of their customers below the level where they would demand a refund.

When we delivered a report showing how to bring balance and control to the company, the blue pill Operations Executive read it, frowned, and dropped it to his desk. His lip practically curled when he said, "Nothing on here makes sense. Our customer service is fine, and our engineering department is stellar. We roll out more products than most of our competitors. Thank you for your time, Gentlemen."

Needless to say, we didn't get the job. Why? We were talking Red Pill language in a blue pill culture. We might have been speaking Lithuanian, because they didn't understand a word of it.

> "The definition of effectiveness is unique to each company."

We chose an extreme case study to highlight two important points. First, blue pill thinking doesn't understand the Red Pill approach. But even more important, the definition of effectiveness is unique to each company.

Culture + Business Value = Effectiveness

It's vital to be completely clear on what your company culture considers effective. Whether you are in a trendy culture, a distorted culture, or a slow-moving traditional culture—your company's definition of effectiveness is the key to your success with projects in that environment. It also affects how you accrue Effectiveness Benjamins and how you spread the Red Pill mindset. You simply cannot succeed if you're shooting at the wrong target—just as we lost the account by assuming we knew this company's view of Business Value.

That was also the problem with this company's PMO. When forming their team, they failed to feed their project managers heaping portions of their recipe for Business Value. Instead, they threw together project managers from various backgrounds and training programs, wound them up, and set them off to blunder through the weeds trying to get control of the chaos in engineering, customer service, and HR while the executives stayed frustrated because their PMO wasn't boosting sales. Their hardworking PMO felt like they couldn't win a losing battle. Thus, the call to us.

The paradox in this instance was the expectation of the leadership that tightening down was the answer for increased effectiveness when the fact was, bolt loosening was what they needed. They needed to become adaptive in order to flow with the Business Value requirements. With a case this extreme, the best tactic might have been to dissolve their PMO and start over with an informal Bare Knuckled Organization who could get in tune with the company's Business Value and grow from there.

Adaptive leadership is integral to the Red Pill model where the parameters expand and contract according to the Business Value Potential. This idea goes directly counter to the blue pill model and becomes a sticking point when bringing a Red Pill presentation to a blue pill audience. That's why dissemination of red pills has to happen organically based on results.

> "Your company's definition of effectiveness is readily visible when you know what to look for."

Determining your own company's definition of effectiveness might seem tricky at first, but it's readily visible when you know what to look for. Take a look around and ask these questions:

What does my company reward?

In our case study, the salespeople drove muscle cars and wore Italian suits. They hung out at country clubs and enjoyed fine dining. Most of the engineers, on the other hand, looked like they had perpetual hangovers, even those who didn't drink. Sales figures were updated several times a day on big white boards in the hallway outside the employee lounge. No one ever mentioned the stats in the other departments—no kudos went in that direction.

Does the company reward speed or a more methodical pace? Do they praise team members who stay organized? Recognize those who grind out mountains of work? Or maybe they reward a perfect safety record with no injuries.

> "If you take notice and take a few notes, you'll soon recognize a pattern."

What topics come up during speeches at awards ceremonies? What's the language on plaques and trophies hanging in the hallways and offices?

If you take notice and take a few notes, you'll soon recognize a pattern.

What does the company spend their budget on?

Money talks. If the company budget has a balloon item, that's a sure indication where their Business Value lies. Which departments get funding and which are always on the short end of the stick? Which projects are underfunded and which have plenty and to spare?

Bonuses and incentives are another place where money talks. If a company is willing to give away its resources to improve performance, they place a high value on that activity.

Once you know your company's perspective on Business Value, you will know how to improve your own effectiveness and how to guide your team toward goals that matter.

Stage 2: Organic Change

Red Pill evolution happens by *growth through cellular division*: where one cell with a DNA mutation reproduces. The Sage has that mutation, and it spreads from person to person, expanding in concentric circles. This is an organic and natural transformation. It sticks because the change happens at the core, all the way down to the limbic brain in System 1.

You cannot simply hold a series of meetings, explain to your team that you've found a new method and expect everyone to get with the program. System 2 cannot reason out the change and have it stick. *Growth through cellular division* means a DNA change that's so primal it cannot give way, even under intense cultural pressure.

In *Edge of Tomorrow*, Rita Vrtaski was the first to take the red pill. She had millions in banked Effectiveness Benjamins since billboards all over the world touted her as the Angel of Verdun. She was a solid warrior, but she got kicked out of the reset system before she became a Sage.

> "Growth through cellular division means change that's so primal it cannot give way, even under intense cultural pressure."

When Cage came up with a strategy to take out the Omega, the one thing he lacked was credibility. So, he cashed in Rita's Benjamins to give himself enough momentum to enroll J Squad.

Notice, Rita didn't take over the mission. She simply gave Cage her credibility.

When Cage passed out red pills, the entire squad took them. At that moment, J Squad became a Red Pill unit under Cage's direction.

No one barked an order. No one set up a PowerPoint presentation showing all the benefits of swallowing the red pill. No one restructured the army to set up squads of Red Pill operatives.

> "They believed, and they followed him."

At the deepest level, J Squad sensed that Cage had become a Sage. They believed, and they followed him. It's as simple as that.

Stage 3: An Informal Red Pill Alliance Forms

As *growth through cellular division* continues, the resulting Red Pill operatives naturally collaborate to get their projects done. Shared beliefs bring them together in a comradery few in the corporate world enjoy. We call this spontaneous group the *Bare Knuckled Organization*. Unhindered by corporate restraint, this team uses Red Pill practices that are simple and direct. Their methods work, so team members share them, and their methods proliferate through the ranks. Bare Knuckled Organizations have a common goal that bonds them together. That goal is effectiveness.

If you are an Operations Executive and a Bare Knuckled Organization emerges in your department, your success rates will rise and your account will swell with effectiveness currency. If you are a project manager in an enterprise that values your results, you'll enjoy greater job security, the security of knowing you can succeed anywhere, regardless of what happens to you in this firm. You will have life security.

Need and crisis are often the driving force behind this motivation for change. In a true emergency, blue pill methods don't work. When a Great White Shark rampages among the tourists, when aliens are about to take over the world, when the company is about to go under, people become more open to trying something new like the Red Pill.

> "Need and crisis are often the driving force behind this motivation for change."

After Cage enrolled J Squad and formed his Bare Knuckled Organization, they set out to blow up the Omega. They had no orders. Their leadership didn't even know they existed. They simply went out and did what needed to be done. If the story had played forward without the reset in the movie, several things could have happened:

1. They could have been heralded as heroes and made an official PMO.
2. They could have been designated as black ops who worked undercover in their bare knuckled status.
3. They could have been disbanded and sent their separate ways to continue practicing the things they learned and spreading the Red Pill perspective.
4. They could have been court martialed.

Company culture determines what a successful outcome looks like. We've said a dozen times before, this is where stuff gets real. Just because you slay the Omega, doesn't mean you're going to get a Gold Star. You might, but then again you might not. If your company doesn't care about the Omega, all your effort could be dismissed as a waste of manpower and time.

In Cage's case, he knew the armies of the world wanted the battle to end. To get that done, the Omega had to die. First get clear on what your company considers Business Value, and only then go after the Omega.

Case Study: Seeding for Change

A few years ago, a privately held financial software company in Philadelphia acquired a legal-research firm in Washington, DC to augment their own Law Research Division. They planned to fold the research company into the Law Division of the Philadelphia parent. After two years of failed attempts, stuff got real. The Philadelphia parent decided to close their Law Division and transfer all products, services, and staff to Washington, DC. It was September. The deadline for the transition was that year's end.

With this complete reversal in direction, the Washington company had to absorb 130 staff, business processes, tools, products and management. Nearly 110 of the staff were regional sales reps scattered across the US and the UK. All staff would be released and given the option to re-apply for employment with the Washington firm.

All personnel actions would be final on January 1, so all technology and operations support must be in-place and ready to go. This date would not slip.

Our client, the CTO, had a lot to do and very little time to get it done. To his credit, he knew he had most of the talent needed to implement the technical changes, but he also knew that most of his project managers were also technical leads who couldn't coordinate across dozens of individual efforts.

As always, culture also came into play. This was a very senior organization, chockfull of experts who rarely gave account for anything other than their single technical focus. They saw communication as unnecessary, since things get done when they get done. They saw coordination as someone else's problem, as in, "If someone needs something from me, they can come and ask for it. Otherwise, it's not my problem."

What was the real challenge? The real challenge was their slow-moving PMO had a tight deadline. They were like the Titanic trying to turn before hitting the iceberg. The CTO knew their ship was about to go down. It was only a matter of time.

To avoid disaster, he called in our team to rapidly convert this blue pill group into a Bare Knuckled Organization.

Remember, a Bare Knuckled Organization cannot be mandated. We didn't need a mandate from the CTO. His situation provided that. We didn't need permission to change PMO standards or governance. We had top-cover from the CTO.

> "A Bare Knuckled Organization cannot be mandated."

To speed up the process, we seeded the organization with Red Pill PMs to get control over these many moving parts and rapidly disseminate the Red Pill mindset.

We started with strategic planning. In a few short hours, we clarified what project success looked like and what Business Value looked like to the CTO. Beyond the Triple Constraints, we got strategic awareness of the CTO's situation, so our Red Pill PMs could provide executive options before he requested them.

We took ownership of the portfolio and set up a Bare Knuckled Organization in the least disruptive manner possible. We identified and prioritized the projects, taking over 50 projects down to four. We separated the roles of Strategic PM and Tactical PM.

The Strategic PMs operated as an extension of the CTOworking in alignment with what he valued along with proactive risk mitigation. This allowed our Tactical PMs to enroll new Red Pill PMs who would remain on the CTO's permanent staff. Minting new Red Pill PMs and removing those of the blue pill persuasion became a force multiplier that worked very well.

However, not everything went swimmingly. Blue Pill senior technical leads suddenly found themselves surrounded by Red Pill PMs who insisted on project discipline. Some of these technical leads went into full revolt and tried to shut us down.

A Red Pill operative expects this type of conflict. It's actually one of the more enjoyable aspects of working with people and turned into a terrific challenge, since we needed those senior technical leads to stay on and perform at their highest level.

A first pass at Red Pill reform will bring out the blind spots and cultural idiosyncrasies. At this point, you can begin to formulate an idea of what this company considers Business Value. In this case, we had a task of moving quickly while the veterans were accustomed to a culture that worked slowly. We didn't see effectiveness as getting behind the tortoise and pushing.

> "A first pass at Red Pill reform will bring out the blind spots and cultural idiosyncrasies."

Instead, we found ways to make them value our different approach. In a few weeks, we went from full-on and open revolt to quiet sidebar conversations where we heard things like, "OK, I get it now. I see what you are doing, and I'm going to try your way." Red pills were easily accessible to everyone, and several of those calloused old skeptics took them.

We turned these technical leads around by providing operational value. That kind of change sticks. Executive pressure or governance cannot effect such lasting change.

The merger arrived at completion on time, within budget and with all planned functional scope in place, a feat nearing the miraculous according to the CTO and his staff. In addition, the CTO had time to elevate project standards so the merger was, in his words, "elegant."

This CTO seeded his company by hiring Red Pill PMs to infiltrate and enroll his personnel. It was the most direct way to quickly bring in the Red Pill model and get the job done.

Although nerve wracking and the cause of sleepless nights, need and crisis are a great catalyst to introduce Red Pill thinking into a company.

> "Impatience can create chaos that ends in disaster."

However, proceed with caution. This is no time for System 1 decisions based on panic and overwhelm. Impatience can create chaos that ends in disaster.

A Case for Patience

With all you've learned throughout this study, the temptation to become a Red Pill evangelist can be strong. Remember your limbic learning. Pause and let System 2 come on board before rushing headlong through your company, megaphone in hand, spreading the good news. When a Red Pill evangelist has no effectiveness currency to anchor the change, spreading the Red Pill message becomes a hypothetical exercise that won't produce results. Strong roots grow only when effectiveness proves this stuff works.

> "Strong roots grow only when effectiveness proves this stuff works."

Red Pill thinking spreads best by example, by demonstrating effectiveness and showing success. As in the case of the Philadelphia company where they had a tight schedule, hiring Red Pill professionals to seed their team sped up the process, but even that transformation took a little time and caused some pain.

Allow your Red Pill team members time to become hardened operators, veterans who know the score and have the experience to mentor their rookie co-workers. Take time to evaluate your new hires, so you're adding qualified people who can make the grade.

After more than a decade working within the Red Pill model, we still carefully consider candidate selection. We've experienced dozens of misfires among our promising new hires. We learn more and more with every fail, but even at that, we still have washouts. So did Marsellus. So did Al Braverman. And so will you.

Case Study: A Startup in Forced Growth

An exception to slow dissemination of the red pill is a new company that experiences rapid expansion and must embrace effectiveness from the start. We worked with an organization like this in Oxford, Pennsylvania, a few years ago.

This company grabbed hold of the Red Pill concept and quickly made it their new normal. The reason: they were a $3MM company who landed a $15MM contract. When the champagne toasts were over, the executive team had an OMG moment realizing they now had to deliver five times the volume they had done in their best year.

This was a case that fell within the 17% of projects that could threaten the very life of the business. The executive team realized that without help, their big win could take their fledgling company down.

They were so new and had hit the ground running so fast, they had never paused to create a culture of effectiveness. Now they found themselves in a state of forced growth and had no choice but to focus on effectiveness. Their culture was open to it. The executives were open to it. They just didn't know how to do it.

They had no time to bring in methodology. They simply did the things that worked and ditched the things that didn't work. As a result, they only knew the good habits of effectiveness. They didn't encounter typical problems more mature companies go through. Young companies like this cut to the chase and don't know anything different.

Effectiveness became their standard, so they recognized ineffective projects very quickly and shut them down. Today, they are a $75MM organization because they have always rewarded effectiveness. They are scaling even further and are now building processes that are more effective. It's not a perfect world. Their culture has several blind spots, but they are on target with effectiveness.

"Once a crisis is over and the dust has settled, the daily work will take on a different quality."

When introducing the Red Pill approach in a crisis-and-need situation, be aware that once a crisis is over and the dust has settled, the daily work will take on a different quality. As you move forward in your Red Pill style, the fevered pitch of saving the company will feel different from launching your next product iteration. When that happens, simple adjustments will help your team embrace the new normal like breaking in a new pair of shoes.

Stage 4: The Bare Knuckled Organization Becomes a Red Pill PMO

In some cases, corporate leadership will realize the power of effectiveness and make plans to validate the Bare Knuckled Organization with sanctioning and governance to create a Red Pill PMO. This is a double-edged sword. On the one hand, sanctioning provides a wide-open door for proliferation of the Red Pill mindset and speed up the process for creating a Red Pill organization.

"Structure can mean stricture."

On the other hand, putting the Bare Knuckled Organization under company structure can feel limiting to those who are used to rapid guerilla tactics. Structure can mean stricture, including red tape and sign-off requirements that slow progress. We will address this in more detail later in the book.

Within all this variety, two components remain constant:
1. Spreading the Red Pill perspective cannot happen by coercion or mandate. It has to happen organically.
2. The Red Pill perspective is not mental assent. It is a change in core beliefs that hold true under pressure.

Each company is unique and each situation is different. That's part of the beauty of it, the challenge of it, and one of our favorite aspects of the Red Pill journey. One thing is certain, with red pills passing through the ranks, a Bare Knuckled Organization will naturally emerge, and it will be effective.

Chapter 7 Summary

- Spreading the Red Pill mindset is an organic process.
- Many companies never formalize a Red Pill PMO.
- The four stages of the Red Pill evolution:

  Stage 1: The Red Pill Operative Becomes a Sage.
  - The definition of effectiveness is unique to each company.
  - A company's definition of effectiveness is readily visible when you ask, *What does my company reward?* and *What does the company spend their budget on?*

  Stage 2: Organic Change: growth through cellular division.

  Stage 3: An Informal Red Pill Alliance Forms as Red Pill operatives naturally collaborate.
  - Seeding a company is an effective way to spread the Red Pill mindset.
  - A Bare Knuckled Organization cannot be not mandated.
  - A first pass at Red Pill reform will bring out cultural idiosyncrasies.
  - Impatience can create chaos that ends in disaster.

  Stage 4: The Bare Knuckled Organization Becomes a Red Pill PMO.

CHAPTER 8

The Indigenous Bare Knuckled Organization

"There are no rules here—we're trying to accomplish something."
~Thomas A. Edison[80]

The evolution of an organic Bare Knuckled Organization is a rare but interesting process. Stepping over corporate structure, this informal task force starts out as a simple alliance based on human connection. It springs from native soil where it is in tune with the local ecosystem. Like plants that flourish in their home turf, so it is with the indigenous Bare Knuckled Organization.

In the corporate environment, the Red Pill operator feels a magnetic draw toward others who are also forward thinking, focused, and innovative—those with enough energy to break through inertia, with an active mind open to new ideas and a strong stomach that can handle large doses of reality.

When a Red Pill Operations Executive calls together a group to discuss a new concept, those with Red Pill energy pop out of the pack. They stay after meetings to discuss Strategic Alignment and pause in the parking lot to bring up thought-provoking questions about Business Value Potential. They might not know Red Pill vocabulary, but they are keyed into the concepts.

Because they are already part of the company, they understand company culture. They have a sense of what will work in their environment and what would cause too much pain. They know where the lines are and the cost of crossing them. Bare Knuckled Organizations have a distinct advantage because they spring to life from within.

A Bare Knuckled Organization can emerge whether the company has an established PMO in place or not. If an established PMO provides sufficient value, the Bare Knuckled Organization can enhance that value. If the PMO fails 70% of the time, the Bare Knuckled Organization could gradually replace it.

The one problem with this natural evolution? It's slow.

_____

"Natural evolution
is slow."

_____

Crisis and need can speed up the process when the company suddenly has a greater tolerance for change. However, a Bare Knuckled Organization formed as part of crisis intervention often experiences fallout after the crisis is over.

Case Study: Epilogue from Seeding for Change

Going back to our case study of the merger within the Legal Research Division of a DC company, our client the CTO saw our Red Pill approach as a godsend to save the merger. He gave us top cover and an open playing field to get the job done. When he saw our Red Pill tactics avert certain disaster and produce elegant results, he became an avid Red Pill Operations Executive. He loved us.

Unfortunately, his company's leadership didn't see it that way. They held on to Their blue pill mindset like a drowning man gripping a lifeguard's neck. The CTO defended us, protected us, and shielded us. At annual meetings, he vehemently justified the budget to keep us on. He was Chuck Wepner, slugging it out and staying on his feet against all odds.

This went on for several years. His protection within that blue pill environment created a pocket of Red Pill operators. We were in the shark cage with hungry Great Whites circling us and watching for their opportunity to take us out. Because of our top cover, we didn't fully realize how hungry those sharks were.

Finally, our CTO grew tired. He wanted less headaches, fewer battles, and a better life.

When a Bare Knuckled Organization works inside a pocket, they are in a precarious situation. Their sponsor must spend hard-earned Credibility Benjamins to keep the team in operation. Whenever those Benjamins disappear—whether through an operative SNAFU or through a change in position—the team will collapse. Jobs will disappear. Contracts will evaporate. Life as they know it will change.

The moment our CTO turned in his resignation letter, our shark cage disappeared. Company leaders didn't care that we had killed the Omega during the merger. They didn't care about our stellar success rates and our focus on Business Value. They saw us as nothing more than an expendable line item on their expense sheet.

They went a step further and made sweet offers to our operators working within their walls and converted them to blue pill operators. In one swoop, we lost several of our best people. The Great White almost ate us alive.

We learned that a Red Pill pocket inside a blue pill company operates with a level of vulnerability. As a result, we rewrote our contracts and built a stronger shark cage. We got more street smarts because that's what Red Pill operators do. They learn and keep on fighting.

A Bare Knuckled Organization that forms with senior executive top cover has more stability and more potential longevity. In a friendly environment, Red Pill alliances organically spread both up and down the food chain. It's interesting to watch the changes within the company as this happens. But even then, surprises still happen.

Case Study: More from "We Learned a Lot"

In our original case study, this company stopped a project before it barely started, and they learned a lot. Over the next few years, they saw an interesting chain of events. They had dismantled the high-priority project we were involved in because the approach didn't work.

No one expected what would happen next. When they brought in a team of Red Pill operators for that project, they inadvertently seeded their company. Without defining it or formalizing it, the Red Pill mindset started to take root in their native soil.

More and more operators—a pocket there and a pocket there—started kicking butt and taking names. They took ownership, went to the back lot and pulled off the gloves. Their supervisors and sponsors rewarded them for getting stuff done. They grew stronger and more confident. Some blue pill operators left.

Eventually, an indigenous Bare Knuckled Organization solidified into a productivity force. No longer a scope activity, project management became a value opportunity. Company project managers routinely boarded hovercrafts and headed for the Omega. Their Operations Executives had coffers bursting with Effectiveness Benjamins, so their credibility felt strong and stable.

This continued until a jar filled with red pills landed on the conference table of the board of directors. Many of them partook. However, when the jar passed the company's senior executives, they said, "No thanks. I'm good."

Within weeks of that meeting, a gap formed.

When the board spotted Business Value Potential, the CEO looked at his personal agenda and diverted those projects. When the board wanted to shift into more Strategic Alignment, their Chief enforced territory protection and toned down the change.

This case study became a fascinating example of what happens when blue pill and Red Pill leaders operate within the same arena. Soon, Red Pill board members saw this reactionary CEO as a damper to the company's profits. Squandered Business Value Potential damaged the board's beloved bottom line.

After several stormy board meetings, they voted to remove the CEO and free the company from its blue pill anchors.

In this case, the company saw major proliferation of the Red Pill mindset throughout the company until, eventually, they became a Red Pill company. Profits immediately reflected this positive change, and the company shifted into hyperdrive. Remaining blue pills were forced to adapt or leave.

That's the difference between Red Pill pockets within the company and full-out Red Pill transformation. Red Pill pockets are a threat within a blue pill company, easily squashed by those who want to coast along maintaining the *status quo*. Proliferation oozes out to create a more homogenous environment that can alter the entire trajectory of the organization.

Red Pill Operations Face More Challenges

Capturing value is more challenging, more complex, and more holistic. That's right, Red Pill operations are more difficult. Neo's choice was: take the blue pill and go back to sleep or take the red pill and save the world. No one said it would be easy.

Red Pill operators welcome the challenge. They feed off their internal drive and thrive on Red Pill comradery. They share the bond with their team members felt by special ops warriors, street cops, and firefighters: they've got each other's backs, and they get stuff done.

Eventually, these backlot fighters naturally form an informal organization we call a Bare Knuckled Organization [BKO]. Whether spoken or unspoken, every BKO has these five components.

"Red pill operators welcome the challenge."

"They interrogate, probe, and challenge every aspect of every project."

1. Opportunity

Every Operations Executive has a sense that each project involves a business opportunity. However, Red Pill operatives in a Bare Knuckled Organization realize they rarely have the complete picture of Business Value Potential, and they commit to understanding as much as possible. They interrogate, probe, and challenge every aspect of every project until the *fidelity in the true value potential* comes into focus.

> "They see the project as evolutionary and push the limits to capture more value."

2. Ownership

Inside the Iron Triangle, blue pill project managers often say, "That's not my job." Those in a Bare Knuckled Organization take a strategic view of each project with a goal of capturing as much Business Value Potential as possible. For example: The technical team is not binary—with only yes and no choices. Instead, they see the project as evolutionary and continuously look for ways to push their limits and capture more value. The same is true of everyone at the three-sided table.

> "Flexibility provides critical maneuverability to those in the driver's seat."

3. Flexible

The terms Triple Constraints and Iron Triangle show the rigidity of the blue pill model. Corralled by time, cost, and scope, the project management team has no freedom to take in more value. The Bare Knuckled Organization has flexibility to expand and contract as their awareness develops.

When more benefit potential appears, they can expand time and budget to capture the value. When cost outstrips the benefit, they can scale back project parameters or cancel it altogether. This flexibility provides critical maneuverability to those in the driver's seat and gives them the ability to create a win more than 90% of the time.

> "Operators in a BKO test, push, and question everything."

4. Tested

Operators in a BKO test, push, and question everything. From the first inception of an idea, they assess the validity of the concept, looking for a reason to cancel before spending company resources. Every step of the way, testing protects the fidelity in the true value potential.

Once an initiative gets off the white board and into planning, Red Pill operators test constraints to see where they fail, come up short, overestimate or under-deliver. They test sponsor perception—albeit gently, respectfully, and with empathy.

They constantly discuss value potential with other BKO members to make the limits as broad as possible. Sometimes this discussion reveals a flaw and potential value collapses. These projects end quickly, before they cost the organization too much.

"Flexibility provides more control."

In Red Pill methodology each individual involved in the project feels at liberty to voice objections and point out misconceptions. Often the individual in the trenches sees practical problems long before those in leadership do. Bare Knuckled Organizations embrace the valuable input of everyone. When Strategic Alignment is the common goal, all members constantly test for misalignment because canceling a project early is also a win.

5. Grounded in the Real World

The scope of a Red Pill project is practical, grounded in real world value. A sponsor sets initial constraints based on their perception of potential value. As the sponsor's awareness changes, so does the scope and so do the constraints. In an interesting paradox, flexibility provides more control. When an operator has this kind of flexibility, the team can control how much value they capture with the goal of pulling in as much as possible.

The full measure of potential business value is rarely found in a project's initial scope. The Red Pill model unlocks unlimited opportunities to acquire more and more value. The scope changes, the constraints change, and projects succeed more than ever. None of this can happen within the rigid walls of the blue pill model.

In the real world, even ventures that fail in terms of time or budget are rarely considered failures by the project sponsor or organization. The actual test of a pass or fail is the amount of resources a project consumed related to the amount of value gained. That takes us right back to the benefit-cost dynamic.

Creating an Informal Bare Knuckled Organization

Working within the limits of your existing situation, you can seed and foster an in-house Bare Knuckled Organization within your team or department. This informal Red Pill organization will recruit, develop, and promote Red Pill members. Without mandate or structure, this group forms because of their common perspective and common goals. They share a comradery that rewards effectiveness within its ranks.

For BKO members, limbic learning is a career strategy. A project manager with this kind of training runs to the fight and becomes unstoppable—the one they call when everyone else runs for cover. These operators understand strategy and tactics. They know where they want to go and what it takes to get there. They make tough calls and follow through, looking reality squarely in the eyes.

Bare Knuckled Organizations are fierce and fearless. They welcome resistance and love going to the back lot to pull off the gloves. They know that fixing a problem is more important than assigning blame. They get stuff done.

Case Study: Pro-Fit—A Bare Knuckled Organization Emerges During Massive Expansion

For about five years, we periodically worked with Pro-Fit, a $20MM company that designed and fabricated fully customizable athletic shoes. They constantly developed such advanced technology that entering their facility meant spending more time in security—both entering and leaving—than you would spend on a visit to the Pentagon.

An aggressive company always looking for growth opportunities, they had a cadre of highly trained project management contractors who worked with them on a regular basis, each with multiple certifications in several methodologies. Pro-Fit would engage our company periodically for special initiatives, such as the launch of a new design or opening a new research facility—projects that were too large or complex for those minding the store.

At the beginning of our relationship, executives would bring us in to save their hides when they got in over their heads. They were blue pill all the way, but once in a while they hired Red Pill operators because they needed effectiveness. The window opened and closed with changing circumstances.

Then a new COO came into the company, a blue pill operator named James Dvorak. James worked on a project with Bryan Wolbert, one of our best operatives. James loved Bryan's effectiveness. Sometime later, he got into a FUBAR situation and called us to say, "I need Bryan."

Bryan got to work and became a Rockstar at Pro-Fit. Suddenly, they wanted more Bryans. During this time, Bryan worked with their team of their regulars and handed out as many red pills as he had takers.

One operator rose above his peers: Bruce Wilkins, a laidback guy who resembled actor Hugh Laurie. Bruce didn't say much, never seemed to be in a hurry, and always dressed like he was about to have lunch with the governor.

Bruce took the red pill from Bryan, along with several others. Red pills operatives were popping up all over James' department. There was blood in the water, and it was spreading fast. Several of our trainers went in and solidified their approach.

A Bare Knuckled Organization organically evolved within that sector of the company. Even with others stepping into the ring, Bruce continued to show his mettle. He went 15 rounds and stayed on his feet. When he needed to, he'd put together a squad and take out the Omega.

Typically, he would meet with James in private, then return to the project management bunker and spread the word from the top. In effect,

Bruce was a Strategic PM, although his official title was simply Project Manager.

Bruce built trust with James to the point that James began sharing the Business Value in a project and the ocean of potential around that value. James handed Bruce the keys to the storeroom, and Bruce responded with effectiveness and reliability. Bruce saw the world through James's eyes. He understood what James wanted, anticipated what James wanted, and knew how to make it happen.

Bruce Wilkins became The Wolf to James Dvorak.

For example, if someone on the team wasn't working out, Bruce didn't wait for the boss to notice. Instead, he'd tell James, "I'm not happy with this person. They aren't working out. I'm going to remove them. Are you okay with that?"

James would offhandedly mutter, "Sure," and move on to the next item of business. And why not? That's what he wanted—a team that works effectively. Bruce said exactly what the Operations Executive would have said, so it was easy for James to nod and say, "Yep." That's a Red Pill operative working in the sweet spot.

Bruce's Benjamins continued to rise. He knew the boss's perspective, so he could anticipate his wishes. This took tons of weight off James. Over time, Bruce became embedded into a leadership role on James's team, though Bruce was still a contractor and still had the same job title.

Bruce gave directions to his peer project managers and watched the work with a keen eye. Whenever a train wreck happened, Bruce took a breath and stepped in with System 2 engaged. He righted the train and had it back on the rails before James got the call.

The trust and open communication between James and Bruce created a strong machine for effectiveness that allowed them to capture even more Business Value Potential as it appeared during a project. They had a great thing going and both of them profited in Effectiveness Benjamins.

Back at the bunker, Bruce had developed an informal structure. He knew the strengths and mindsets of his peer project managers. He recognized his fellow Red Pill teammates and shared strategic information with them. He also knew which project managers were stolid blue pill traditionalists and left them to their box-ticking activities.

This informal BKO happened organically. Because it formed as an indigenous part of the company, it cannot be dismantled and still runs to this day. If Bruce experienced a lifechanging event that caused him to leave the company, James would immediately look within the ranks for someone else to fill that leadership position, someone Bruce has already groomed for the job. The BKO would live on.

After more than a year of this, James told our team, "Maybe I need to be more Red Pill myself. How would I do that?"

We said, "Create a little more framework around Bruce. Fill a Petri dish with Red Pill nutrients that empower your operators. Nurture a Red Pill team that knows how to get stuff done and make you look good in the process."

That's exactly what happened. Bruce got a new title: Strategic Project Manager, which gave him more authority. Their BKO advanced to new levels of effectiveness, and James started piling up even more Benjamins. He used this currency to build more Red Pill operators around him.

In a perfect world, we'd like to say that James turned his sector into a Red Pill arena where pushback and Strategic Alignment are the order of the day. However, in some areas James is still blue pill. He works within a blue pill environment and doesn't have the cultural flexibility to bring the company or even his own department into a pure Red Pill model.

James can't go into a phone booth, pull off his shirt and become the Red Pill Hero in cape and tights. He has to be coy and make suggestions. He has to push a little and bide his time.

Real world scenarios aren't pristine. They are often dirty and sometimes downright ugly. The Pro-Fit environment often gets wonky. People wade into the mud and slug it out once in a while. Whatever the realities of their day-to-day operations, James's department is massively effective compared to where they were when we first met them back in 2013.

One of the situations James was up against is that Valerie Wakefield, the president of the company, had different values. Yes, she wanted to grow the company's bottom line, but her WIIFM (What's In It For Me) also included political clout and personal advancement within government circles. She would sanction a project that was out of Strategic Alignment to the company's purpose if that project gave her a chance to grow political capital.

This caused some tension for James, whose first impulse was to set Valerie straight. However, she was his superior, and she frankly didn't care. James had to work within Valerie's parameters while he tried to stay in Strategic Alignment as much as possible. For this reason, the Bare Knuckled Organization at Pro-Fit might never become formalized into a Red Pill PMO.

And that's totally okay.

Company culture creates an operational framework. When leadership doesn't agree on what constitutes effectiveness, the culture contains tension and a pain threshold that can't withstand too much pressure. We quickly learned to color inside the lines while working at Pro-Fit.

> "Company culture creates an operational framework."

For James, effectiveness meant one thing: growing the company's Business Value. For Valerie, effectiveness meant building her political standing by doing favors for strategic people in return for "I owe you one" relationships. Sure, she wanted to grow the company and keep her job, so she often brought in deals that accomplished both goals.

James's currency was so different from Valerie's that they could not trade with each other any more than you can spend pesos at a sidewalk café in Shanghai. Valerie saw James's Benjamins as on a level with baby wipes, and James saw hers as worse than that. They could not deal in trade. They had to work around each other.

When we sent our people to work with Pro-Fit, they had to adjust to this distinction. Those working with James had one flavor of effectiveness— let's call it vanilla—while those working with Valerie had a different flavor—vanilla with sprinkles. Trained to line up with the perspective of the project sponsor, our operatives gave each of these leaders what they wanted. As specialized contractors, our own Benjamins depended on working within the company's cultural tension as well. We weren't there to crusade. We were there to get stuff done.

In 2016 Pro-Fit landed a contract with the US military that would expand their company twentyfold virtually overnight. Using proprietary technology, Pro-Fit would produce insoles that were soft, absorbent, and flexible while also holding the foot completely stable. These insoles would go inside the boots of every soldier in the US Army infantry. If they worked well, the order would expand throughout the Army and to the other branches as well.

This was the motherlode.

The caveat: they had to deliver their first shipment in four months. That's when they called us. Crisis and need often open the door for Red Pill operations.

If you're a Red Pill Operations Executive who wants someone like Bruce on your team, simply seeing the world with new eyes will help you shift your effectiveness to a higher gear. You want a lieutenant to take some of the weight off. You want a team that leans into the fight and brings home the prize.

"Crisis and need often open the door for Red Pill operations."

However, before you take any action, spend some time considering on your own flavor of effectiveness. Are you on board with the *fidelity in the true value potential* as defined by your company's purpose and mission? What's your own WIIFM? Can you get what you want while also staying in fidelity? How would that work?

What flavor is your effectiveness?

James saw staying in Strategic Alignment with the company's mission as a way to grow his resume and build his career. His own desires lined up with the company's mission and that gave him momentum. His numbers showed it.

Valerie's WIIFM had a double agenda: political clout plus company mission. She was shooting at a target with two bullseyes. Sometimes they overlapped and sometimes they didn't, so her aim had some wobble in it. As long as she achieved enough Strategic Alignment to satisfy her superiors, she kept on going.

When you are the Operations Executive or project sponsor, you can order your favorite flavor of effectiveness. That's the home team advantage.

However, when stuff gets real—and it will—it's critical that you are clear. What does your ocean of value look like? What is your fidelity in the true potential value? How do you define a win?

Valerie's flavor of effectiveness meant keeping her friends in high places happy. Her team scrambled and worked weekends, even with unreasonable deadlines and near-impossible requirements. Those extreme measures cost the company thousands, but for Valerie the relationship benefit made the dollar cost worth it.

It's interesting that Bryan also worked with Valerie, and she also thought he was a Rockstar. Why? He got clear on her flavor of effectiveness, and he delivered. That's what it means to be a Red Pill operator.

> "Shape behaviors by rewarding effectiveness."

How can you encourage an effective BKO within your department or organization? Create a Petri dish filled with the nutrients that produce powerful Red Pill operators. Shape behaviors by rewarding effectiveness and see who rises to the occasion using these elements:

- Encourage initiative, not just meeting requirements.
- Inspire ownership.
- Emphasize Strategic Alignment.
- Set the compass toward Business Value.
- Use Limbic Learning to see who makes solid decisions under intense pressure.
- Foster open, honest discussion.
- Consider killing a useless endeavor as a win for the team.
- Teach everyone to stay on their own side of the three-sided table.

- Reward effectiveness.

Let them feel the benefits of accumulating Benjamins and develop a taste for acquiring more and more.

As you pass the jar of red pills around the table, those with insight and resourcefulness will soon separate themselves from the drones. Before long, you'll recognize the ones with potential to become The Wolf. Test them, train them, develop them. Throw them opportunities and watch their responses.

> "Reward according to what is effective rather than what is required."

You know what to do. The real question is whether you want to spend a lot of time and energy developing your indigenous BKO slowly through organic gardening, or whether you want to speed thing up by bringing in Red Pill contractors and trainers to seed your department, water, and prune.

Either way, once you have your Red Pill lieutenant in place, task them with identifying others who have the same capability. Hire staffing company that can identify a Red Pill to bring you more people who are Red Pill material. You can take this as far as the culture allows.

Before you begin, consider these questions:

- Are you creating a pocket of Red Pill operatives using your top cover as protection or seeding entire the company?
- Will initiating a Red Pill movement require you to spend your own Effectiveness Benjamins and keep spending them to maintain it?
- How much energy will you need to establish momentum?

Beware of overzealous action. First, it rarely works and, second, you could end up a casualty of your own unbridled enthusiasm. Push the culture too hard and it might snap back... on you.

Chapter 8 Summary

- An organic Bare Knuckled Organization starts out as a simple alliance based on human connection.
- A Bare Knuckled Organization can emerge whether the company has an established PMO in place or not.
- Natural evolution is slow, but crisis and need can speed up the process.
- Red Pill operations face more challenges because capturing value is more complex.
- Every BKO has these five components:
  1. Opportunity
  2. Ownership
  3. Flexible
  4. Tested
  5. Grounded in the Real World
- Bare Knuckled Organizations share a comradery that rewards effectiveness within its ranks.
- A BKO that forms as an indigenous part of the company cannot be dismantled.
- Company culture creates an operational framework.
- Shape behaviors by rewarding effectiveness and see who rises to the occasion.
- Let your team feel the benefits of accumulating Benjamins and develop a taste for acquiring more and more.

CHAPTER 9

The Secret Ingredient

"You've made just enough safe choices to stay alive, but not enough to matter. Is that what you want? You can be more. You want to be more, don't you?"

~Joe MacMillan in *Halt and Catch Fire*[81]

> ### *Halt and Catch Fire*[82]
> Starring Lee Pace, Scoot McNairy, and Mackenzie Davis
> AMC Studios, 2014
>
> *Halt and Catch Fire* is an American period drama television series that aired on AMC network from June 1, 2014, to October 14, 2017. A fictionalized story about the evolution of the computer, in its first season the series covers the invention of the PC.
>
> For our purposes we focus on the first eight episodes from Season One. When Joe MacMillan (Lee Pace) leaves IBM to join Cardiff Electric, he spearheads Cardiff's

expansion into the world of the PC along with hardware engineer Gordon Clark (Scoot McNairy) and software programming prodigy Cameron Howe (Mackenzie Davis). Although filmed in Atlanta, the first season of the series is set in the Silicon Prairie of Dallas-Fort Worth.

Up until now, we've talked about the Red Pill mindset and how it increases your effectiveness. We've discussed Strategic Alignment vs. WIIFM, value potential vs. task completion, rigid constraints vs. adaptive flexibility, resume qualifications vs. effectiveness, and understanding brain chemistry. While all are valid and essential, one element holds all of them in a container so strong yet so invisible, it's like a glass fishbowl. It's funny how the fish can't really see it, but it rules their life just the same.

That secret ingredient is culture.

Red Pill operatives develop a sensitivity to culture. They know how to identify the walls provided by organizational culture and learn to ride patterns or flow. Like the EAC[83] current in the animated movie *Finding Nemo*, if the operative can find her balance and catch a ride on open culture-currents—*Cowabunga, Baby!* However, blunder in unawares and she could also end up smashed on the rocks.

Culture controls everything. Culture dictates tolerance for change. Culture dictates how much pushback the upper echelon of the company will allow. Culture dictates what is said and unsaid in meetings. Culture sets the tone of communications and decides who gets access to information. It has no pity on the weak and no patience for the incompetent.

Culture flows where it wants, and it's ruthless.

"Culture has no pity on the weak and no patience for the incompetent."

In *Halt and Catch Fire*, visionary Joe MacMillan enrolls inventor Gordon Clark into staging an innovation coup on Cardiff Electric. A former IBM* employee, Joe sees a vast ocean of Business Value Potential. Cardiff has the manpower and technology to harvest that potential. Gordon has the skills and experience to manage the project and oversee the hardware development.

Joe and Gordon spend a weekend deconstructing the code on an IBM® machine. They create a magnificent plan a with blinking light on the top of the package called global opportunity.

Life is messy. Dealing with people gets down and dirty. If you're an Operations Executive you've been there and done that. You know what we're talking about.

At their three-sided table, Joe has first chair as the sponsor, and Gordon fills the second chair as the project manager (with his hand in the hardware technology as well). Gordon works in a war room with a team of technicians who are in the third chair at the table. In the beginning, this looks like a Red Pill three-sided table. However, setting the table doesn't guarantee a Red Pill outcome.

> "Life is messy. Dealing with people gets down and dirty."

Also, in the third chair is software genius Cameron Howe. Cameron is rude with little concern about grooming or professional behavior. She's so single-minded about launching this new computer system, she works around the clock. She writes an operating system from scratch without cracking their book of deconstructed code.

Cameron is also street smart. She drives a hard bargain and beats her own drum. No one can tame her.

Joe has a pseudo-red-pill mindset at the outset, but he soon reveals himself as blue pill. Although he's focused on Business Value with this project, he's actually working for a hidden agenda, protecting his ego and guarding his turf—blue pill all the way.

VP John Bosworth (played by Toby Huss) is the quintessential blue pill boss. When IBM® shows up on Cardiff's door with a cadre of pricey lawyers, John turns fifty shades of purple. He wants to fire Joe and Gordon and anyone else who walks through his line of sight. However, with Cardiff facing the biggest lawsuit in the company's history, their only recourse is to play out Joe's carefully crafted rebuttal. John has to let them proceed or the company admits culpability.

Held off by Cardiff's strategic play, IBM° goes on the warpath and raids Cardiff's clientele—offering deals no one can match. Before long, the only game left at Cardiff is Joe's brainchild computer system.

Despite all this upheaval and drama, the project moves forward, until even John Bosworth realizes the Business Value Potential within their grasp. He gets behind it despite intense pressure from the blue pill owner of the company. Eventually, John mortgages his house and puts his own cash on the line when the company faces bankruptcy, and they need an investor.

Cameron works alone in a dark basement until she launches the operating system. Downstairs in that cave where she's completely unaware of day or night, she gives birth through hard labor, sweat, and tears. She emerges from the darkness forever changed. Now she has one purpose: to keep her baby alive and well, no matter what.

Joe sends Cameron off on vacation. When she comes back, she finds the company reorganized. When she steps through the door to the hardware room, she hears the guys discussing names for the system. Her response: "I wrote the BIOS. I name it. Lovelace." Mama Cameron isn't about to let someone else name her baby. This is her child. She feels it down to the bone.

Cameron's iron-clad mission covers the entire organization. If her baby is to thrive, everyone in the company has to align with its best interest. She no longer sees herself as an employee drawing a paycheck. She is a force. Cameron is now the culture of the company.

> "As with Cameron, company purpose and mission are intractable and ruthless."

As with Cameron, company purpose and mission are intractable and ruthless. Those who set the tone for the working parts and people interactions are likewise intractable and ruthless. "For the good of the company" becomes the mantra. Individuals might be mowed down—from the janitor to the president of the board—but the company lives on. This is culture.

Woe to anyone who challenges culture head on. Any shifts must be nuanced and incremental. Motivation for change must come from within the culture itself. We've seen it time and time again. Challenge culture at your peril. We can't emphasize it enough.

But there's more...

Cameron's new supervisor is blue pill leader, Steve. He's a newcomer and has no idea what happened in the basement. With a dismissive attitude, he assigns Cameron to a cubicle in the middle of a room filled with software programmers.

She holds back for a little while, getting her bearings before she takes action.

Things come to a head when Steve patronizingly asks Cameron, "Did you check off your module on the flowchart?"

She retorts, "No, I just told you I'm finished."

He says, "Well, I still need you to put a check by your name. It's part of the protocol. Learned it at Stanford B School."

She bursts out, "Does the B stand for bull----?"[84]

With that shot over the bows, Cameron continues to bide her time.

Working in the software room, Cameron notices an informal alliance of programmers who know how to get stuff done. They toss each other tips and quips over the cubical walls and share a geeky camaraderie around a computer game called *Adventure*. She quickly identifies them as the most effective members of the team.

Eventually, Cameron has enough of all the blue pill shenanigans. It's time for culture to speak out.

She heads for Joe's office. Steve follows her. Here's how the scene plays out [with our notes in brackets]:

Cameron says to Joe: "Hey, do you want to have all of your software programmed in 11 weeks for half of what you're spending?"

[Culture's objective is launching the system as fast as possible. She wants to know if Joe has Strategic Alignment with her goal because she's about to unleash culture as a tool.]

Joe MacMillan looks up from his paperwork and asks, "Is this a trick question?"

Cameron says: "Brooks' law. *The Mythical Man-Month*: the one useful book I read in college. Brooks said that adding programmers to speed up a software project only makes it later."

Steve says: "She's got a real attitude problem."

[Blue pill Steve wants only process compliance. He can't hear culture's primal need for speed.]

Cameron notices Steve. "Oh! Also, I'm taking over Steve's job."

Steve smirks. "See what I mean?"

Joe: How would you know which programmers to keep? Do you even know their names?

Cameron yells into the programming room, "Hey! (whistles) Coder-monkeys, come here! How many of you got sucked into *Adventure* last night?"

Every programmer raises their hand.

Steve says, "I knew it! She's sabotaging the project, Joe!"

She just shoved Steve's business school approach right in his ear, and he never sees it coming. Obsession with formulas creates operators who are blue pill blind to culture. Only pulling off the gloves and going to the back lot will allow you to see it, one small step at a time.

> "Obsession with formulas creates operators who are blue pill blind to culture."

Cameron asks the geeks which of them cracked the code to get out of the cave. Three raise their hands. After another question, Cameron tells Joe to keep those three and send the rest home. If these three geeks are good enough to crack the code on *Adventure,* they can finish the project ahead of time.

Joe says: "Steve, I'll write you a nice letter of recommendation."[85]

Challenge culture, and, like Steve, you'll land on the curb before you know what hit you.

Blue pill thinkers like Joe and Steve default to structure, rules, and processes because that's what they understand.

Cameron is neither blue pill nor Red Pill. She simply wants to keep her baby healthy, so the most effective team is the one she supports. You might think you are Red Pill. Don't kid yourself.

No one is Red Pill in this story. That's the point. Cultures and organizations can be a real mess, yet still be growing, progressing, even profitable.

It's up to Red Pill operators to recognize and inform culture and slowly modify it for better effectiveness.

Red Pill or blue pill: Which are you?

Loosely, there are four types of operators.

1. Blue Pill[86]

With blind adherence to formulas, the blue pill operator divides everything into two categories: either it fits inside process lines or it doesn't. If it doesn't, they refuse to play ball. We've seen multi-million-dollar initiatives collapse because of this one blue pill trait. Blue pill operators are rigid in triple constraint requirements and focus on project completion rather than Business Value. They do what's required rather than what is effective, and they simply react to culture without ever seeing culture. This creates process adherence to absurdity.

A few years ago, we needed a timeline to set up our milestones and deadlines. Our client's blue pill shop refused to give us any dates. Their process didn't allow for schedules. Even the president of the business couldn't get them to deliver something that simple. Our company had to withdraw, and a project with massive Business Value Potential ended before it began. Worse, they got away with it. That's blue pill constriction. It kills creativity and innovation and does not adapt to change.

1. Red Pill Posers[87]

The Red Pill poser likes the effectiveness of Red Pill operators, but they are blue pill blind to culture. They don't understand that core beliefs are the foundation for Red Pill power, not a series of learned practices. When pushed, they revert back to blue pill tactics—choosing personal agendas rather than Strategic Alignment and taking action for reasons other than Business Value Potential. As a result, they have no Effectiveness Benjamins. A poser has a double standard and that makes them an open target for a culture slap.

2. Immature Red Pill[88]

New Red Pill operators get so excited about their expanded thinking, they easily slip into crusader mode, trying to convince blue pill people to change. These rookies are still stretching to adapt to Red Pill methods. They have studied Limbic Learning but still slip into overwhelm. They know the value of Strategic Alignment but still struggle to identify whether a specific project aligns or not. They feel awkward at speaking out and pushing back. Always keen to show their mettle and collect Effectiveness Benjamins, sometimes they come off as over-eager. In best-case scenarios, the immature Red Pill person works with a coach or mentor.

As with any novice, assimilating the basic components of Red Pill methods means focus and practice over time. They have to think about what they're doing to make it happen, and mistakes are part of the learning process.

3. Mature Red Pill[89]

The veteran Red Pill operator sees the battle as recognizance mission. Always seeking better ways to be effective, every operation provides more understanding of culture. Every success opens the way for more effectiveness, and every resistance reveals cultural limitations.

Seasoned in the flow of change and adaptation, the mature Red Pill person encourages creativity and innovation to capture more Business Value Potential. They embrace culture and know how to harness its power. They subtly adjust cultural trends within the organization and examines every project idea for a cultural fit. They have a hefty stash of Effectiveness Benjamins and understand when to remain silent and when to speak out.

Where the Immature Red Pill operator has to focus to stay on track, the Mature Red Pill operator rides cultural currents, adjusting for tilt and momentum. He calmly follows the guidance of Air Traffic Control until their instructions won't work. Then, he pushes back. The Mature Red Pill operator knows how to land the Airbus A320, even if he has to do it on the Hudson River.

Like Jordan Peterson in *12 Rules for Life*[90], Mature Red Pill operators always push the boundaries of effectiveness. Every day they try to achieve a little bit more, a little bit faster, a little bit better. Like compound interest over a long time, one day they look around and realize they are swimming in a cultural fishbowl. They see the underground currents, the eddies and the flow patterns. Like the board of the company who said, "We learned a lot," they eventually see blue pill leadership as an anchor, launch a cultural coup and summarily discharge its CEO.[91]

Blue pill operators never see culture. If they did, they wouldn't focus on what they focus on, and they wouldn't do what they do.

Going back to Cameron, blue pill operators watch her and say, "Cameron is out of line. She needs to be squashed." Red pill operators see her and say, "That's culture. That's how this

> "Blue pill operators never see culture."

company grapples with survival. Let's see how we can help her get what she wants."

Until you go through what we've described, until you follow through and make incremental improvements to increase effectiveness, until you find the blue walls and bump against the glass fishbowl, you won't fully understand the company culture. It's not in the operations manual or on a poster across the wall of the lunch room. It's the energy left hanging in the air after a meeting's over. It's the movements of people in and around your organization. It's in the flow of information, or the lack thereof.

Culture trumps operations. Always. Everywhere. That's the core reason most companies disband or reorganize their PMOs again and again. Although their blue pill operators work hard to complete their processes and hit their milestones, culture demands more.

> "Culture trumps operations."

Yes, Red Pill operators are effective, but they also have cultural awareness.

Beware the Blue Pill Red Herring

In the beleaguered world of project management, an effective Bare Knuckled Organization will attract attention. Sometimes, the response of blue pill leadership will be to harness that BKO power and try to control it. It's what they do.

Blue pill executives might recognize the un-official BKO and reward it by making it an official and sanctioned organization. They look like they are becoming Red Pill when they embrace the idea of formalizing the BKO as a PMO or larger-scope EPMO (Enterprise Project Management Organization). In reality, they may be applying their blue pill rules to a Red Pill operation. They want to contain it and keep it in a box. That's a blue pill trap!

Integrating a Red Pill entity into corporate structure creates a laundry list of encumbrances, distractions, and responsibilities. You'll have a higher degree of accountability for things that don't matter when it comes to what culture values and more blue pill project initiatives to sift through instead of the critical, strategically derived ones.

If you take on all of this too soon, you'll create a snarl of issues that threaten your Red Pill existence. No more guerrilla moves. You stand in a wide-open field in the glaring sun, and it's hunting season. A prematurely formalized Red Pill organization sometimes doesn't have a chance.

Department walls often insulate the traditionally formed PMO from vital information about Business Value Potential and Strategic Alignment. The more middle men, the more the operator must test and push people who don't want to be tested and pushed. The more layers between you and the person you need to connect with, the more

> "I didn't say it would be easy, Neo. I said it would be the truth."
> ~**Morpheus in** *The Matrix*[114]

people will mess with your aim and the less chance you'll have of hitting the target. Where an unofficial Red Pill operator can stop by the office of a strategic person, sanctioned groups have official channels and chains of command.

That's what bureaucratic red tape is, right? It deflates momentum and takes any project off track with multi-layered agendas and flawed perspectives.

When a blue pill executive talks about incepting a traditional PMO, they are looking at it through a different lens than the culture. They might be looking through a power lens or an operational lens or some other lens. So, when the blue pill executive suggests creating an PMO, the Red Pill operator sees this as a bid for outside control which may or may not be a positive move forward. Formalizing the PMO means putting on the company uniform, and those guerilla combat boots are going to pinch bad.

An immature Red Pill operator sees the change as an advancement because it includes a title and recognition. A Mature Red Pill operator knows better.

A Red Pill operator can work with a blue pill executive who has high motivation for more effectiveness, and the operator might be able to negotiate a Red Pill solution and initiate a Red Pill infusion into that organization. That might move culture to expect more efficient and strategically aligned execution.

If an executive insists on incepting the PMO in a blue pill culture, the Red Pill operator can push the culture a little bit more. But what you have is more of a takeover, not a promotion. This happens all the time.

Case Study: Executive with Silos

We've seen similar scenarios many times. To simplify, we combined them into one case study with a fictious client named Zach.

Zach was a highly creative innovator. He sees his department as his fiefdom and his main objective is to bring his creative ideas to life. He has little regard for governance and regularly circumvents his own system, particularly when he knows one sector of his department won't deliver. In that case, he'll go around them and give special initiatives to someone else.

As a result, he inadvertently creates silos. People in his department are highly protective of their turf and intensely guarded.

When our team went in, they found blue walls all over the place. Our executive advisor finally told Zach, "You're part of the problem."

Immediately Zach went into an irate rebuttal: "No way I can be the problem!" He didn't believe our assessment because—with typical blue pill blindness—he's not seeing his corporate culture.

When Zach said he wanted improvements in effectiveness, the only way to move those blue walls enough to see results was to get Zach to agree to a governance model he didn't like. Actually, he hated it.

However, because we had Benjamins, our executive advisor was able to convince Zach to agree to the plan. Zach was willing to tolerate a new governance model because he wanted effectiveness more than the *status quo*.

We boxed him in, putting constraints around the activities of his group, so they can get more effectiveness despite their twisted culture. Over time, hopefully Zach will admit the change worked and his awareness of his own culture will mature. If he blows it up, he'll have to ask himself the question, *Why did I blow it up?* Whatever happens, he is more likely to advance in his understanding of culture.

Regardless of future developments with Zach, our team wins. We can deliver more effectiveness to Zach as long as it lasts. Because we're consultants we have more power to pull a move like this one. An internal person might play it differently because they have a job on the line.

Push too hard and the culture will pull away from you to relieve the pressure. Push too hard and Zach will feel like a hostage. Before long, he'll lose his creative drive. The box around Zach has to give him enough room to keep his juice going. That's the fine line we walk as Red Pill operators.

How do we find the line?

The Red Pill operator gently pokes the tiger, testing for response. When it snaps, the Red Pill says, "OK, I see where the walls are. Now, let me try something different." No disappointment or anger, this is research. Both results provide information for the next foray, and the fight goes on.

> "The Red Pill operator gently pokes the tiger, testing for response."

Contrast this approach and the blue pill approach that sees only rules, processes, exceptions, or bureaucracies.

Blue pill thinking says sanctioning a Red Pill BKO into an official PMO is the next logical step. Becoming official means integrating a new entity into your corporate structure. This creates a laundry list of encumbrances, distractions, and responsibilities that are largely blue pill driven. You also have a broader and more formal scope of mission such as tool selection, apprenticeship, training, strategic and tactical approaches, process adherence, rapid control of crisis management, strategic alignment, and a whole host of other responsibilities. There's nothing anti-Red Pill about this broader mission, but you need to be ready to lead it.

No longer guerillas working in the tall grass and dodging sentries in the dark, you'll have systems and processes to support your Red Pill operations. You'll have a higher degree of accountability and deal with more ideas for initiatives as you look for maximum Business Value Potential. You'll also have army generals questioning your every move and decision.

People, you're not in Kansas anymore. If you institute a Red Pill PMO before the culture is ready, and as importantly, before you are ready, you'll be in for the biggest, messiest project of your life. More than likely, you'll take a knockout punch and faceplant in front of the whole crowd. Fifty percent of all Project Management Offices disband within just three years.[92] It doesn't get more real than this. Yes, you can do it, but you have to be ready.

> "Institute a Red Pill PMO before the culture is ready and you'll be in for the biggest, messiest project of your life."

Get yourself a trainer who shouts in your ear while you pummel the 100-pound heavy bag until your arms give out. Scale those long stairs every morning for a year or two. Staying on your feet for 15 rounds isn't enough. You'll have to take down the heavyweight champ before he takes you down. But you can't do it with one roundhouse punch.

You're dealing with people and that means politics, unclear thinking, mistakes, oversights, poor budget planning, and the list goes on. Unless your own conviction is rock solid and the culture is fully prepared, your premature Red Pill PMO will probably derail before it leaves the station.

An Ancient Allegory

A famous account from ancient writings dating back to 1000 BC shows this concept beautifully. In the story, David was youngest child in a large family of boys. Always smaller than the others, David got the worst jobs. He tended the sheep, and he was the family gopher sent to fetch and carry whenever someone needed something.

His big brothers served in the army. Because they had titles and brass nameplates on their desks, they thought they were much more effective than little brother David.

David was a fighter in his own right. While out in the fields with the family's flock of sheep, he went hand-to-hand with first a lion and then a bear to protect his flock… and he won. He could run like the wind and he had a steady aim with his sling.

He came from a tribe of fierce warriors known as the Israelites. His family had conquered the entire region about 400 years earlier and had defended it from all attackers ever since. By the time our story begins, the Israelites had generational farms and big families with a deep-rooted love for the land.

The story opens with the Israelites at war. The fight was at a standoff with both armies lined up alongside a valley. Every day during morning prayers, a seasoned soldier roughly the size of Yao Ming would come out from the enemy's camp and taunt the Israelite army. He'd bellow across the valley asking for a one-on-one fight, a contest to determine the winner of the battle.

The Israelite king was about the size of Tony Robbins—a big man compared to everyone else around—but he still looked small compared to that massive soldier and his equally massive sword. For days on end, this had been going on. No one in the Israelite army would volunteer to take on that guy. In their minds, it was certain suicide.

Unaware of all the drama at the battlefront, David loaded food onto some pack mules and headed to the army camp. When he arrived, he heard the big guy shouting from the valley. David rode into camp, looking around to see who would step out and take the challenge, but everyone had their heads down sorting through emails and filling out reports. No one seemed to notice the dire situation playing out right in front of them.

When he reached his brothers, David leapt from his saddle and demanded, "Why aren't you going out to fight that guy?" An argument broke out, and soon David had an angry crowd around him. About the size of Tom Cruise or Elijah Wood, David was one of the smallest in the group, but he didn't care. He reminded them of their culture. They were a tribe of conquerors. They didn't back down for anyone. Ever.

The king heard the commotion and sent for David. In the meeting, David talked about their families and the children back home. He talked about the land of their fathers. He talked about effectiveness and his stash of Benjamins in fighting the wild lion and the bear. David was a Red Pill warrior in the middle of a blue pill tribe.

The king was impressed. He thought, *This guy knows how to be effective. He has the courage to speak out and the heart to follow through. We need that around here.* So, the king decided to give David a sanctioned position in the army. He said, "You're hired. But first you have to put on armor like everyone else."

David was a guerilla fighter, hiding behind rocks and trees then dashing out to get the job done. He fought bare knuckled and did whatever it took to win. But… this was the king, and no one argued with the king. David put on the armor.

However, when he put it on, he could hardly lift his arms. He couldn't dodge and sway. He certainly couldn't run. He went to endless meetings for long discussions that left him feeling so drained, he had no energy left to fight. He spent more time writing reports and preparing presentations than making real progress.

Meanwhile, their noisy enemy kept shouting.

This wasn't working. David took the armor off and told the king, "I'm not ready for armor yet. I haven't practiced in it. Let me work the way I'm effective. Otherwise, I'll be like everyone else, failing 70% of the time."

On the morning of the battle, the big guy came out as usual. When he saw David, he laughed and made all kinds of threats. David ignored him. He loaded his sling, sprinted toward the enemy and fired. That day, he won the battle in less than two minutes.

Why? Because he knew his effectiveness lay in his ability to be nimble and quick. He saw the advantage in his informal approach. That's where he had gained all his Benjamins in the past, and that's where he would continue to accumulate more.

So, when the king of your company comes to you with offers of armor and a heavy sword, beware. It's probably a trap. The shiny suit will make you look good to the guys in the neighborhood, but you'll be weighed down with walls and rules and processes, reporting *ad nauseum*, and governance committees. You'll have a blue pill brace around your Red Pill heart. Nobody can win a fight on the back lot wearing that.

If you find yourself in a situation like David—and if you're effective, you probably will—here are some strategies for warding off a blue-pill coup on your Red Pill BKO:

1. Know it's coming. Begin your game plan long before the situation comes up.
2. See the signs. Notice the warning signals that leadership is starting to think in these terms.
3. Use it as a tool to strengthen your position. The dialogue could go something like this:

   Blue pill Executive: "We should get you guys official, set up an official PMO."

   Red Pill Operator: "All right, but, you know what, I don't believe the process will work the way that you're saying. The processes we have now are ultra-effective and nimble, and we don't want that to change, do we?"

   Blue: "No."

   Red: "If you want to move in the direction of a Red Pill PMO, let's start by injecting the organization with more Red Pill operators and I'll train and mentor them. Let's build an informal team that succeeds with every project and then get them ready to be more formal."

   Blue: "What? We can't do that."

   Red: "Sure. We're not ready to be official yet. Maybe we need to continue acting informally for a while and accumulate more currency first, or we'll likely make things worse instead of better."

If leadership won't accept your feedback and insists on sanctioning, the ball goes back into your court. Can you live within new strictures and take on the slow process of influencing the culture? Are you ready to stand in the wide-open field in the glaring sun? Or… maybe you have enough Benjamins to find a more red-pill-friendly opportunity somewhere else.

The Emergence of a Red Pill Organization

Launching a Red Pill Organization or even a formal PMO is not a quick and easy process. Taking advantage of culture, a Red Pill Organization emerges in 3 Evolutions:

1. Operational Capture Mode. The company begins as a traditional blue pill organization, operating within the rigid Triple Constraint model where success depends on staying within the iron walls of time, budget, and scope/quality. At some point, someone within the company—usually an Operations Executive or project manager—takes the red pill. They want more effectiveness, and they aren't afraid to take off the gloves and go to the back lot. They make a commitment to stay on their feet for 15 rounds, even when stuff gets real. At this earliest stage, with minimal training and few process changes, success rates already begin to rise. Effectiveness is now the goal, so how they measure success begins to change.

2. Value Capture Mode. Hungry for more Business Value, the Red Pill warrior enrolls promising operators into Red Pill value capture mode. Here the Triple Constraints expand and contract throughout a project, so the team can capture more Business Value as it appears. With training and experience over time, Red Pill PMs become Sages and coach others. More Red Pill warriors pull off their gloves and get into the fight. With more flexibility, project success rates continue to increase. New measurement criteria shift the focus to Business Value, so success rates rise even more. Momentum builds.

3. Operational Excellence Mode. Red Pill effectiveness leads to cultural change. Leadership openly shares value potential to the entire Red Pill Organization or PMO. All operators fight for maximum capture. The Red Pill model shuts down unworthy projects before they waste company resources. Red Pill thinking spills into other departments until effectiveness becomes company currency, and the business maintains its upward trajectory.

Notice that in every evolution, culture determines what happens, and what happens next. Sure, insightful operations executives can encourage the process, but culture designs the organization piece by piece, not executives—regardless of whether they are Red Pill or blue pill.

> "Culture designs the organization piece by piece, not executives."

As the Red Pill operator matures, the rookie compulsion to sanction an PMO melts away. Effectiveness has been the goal all along, and effectiveness needs to have room to maneuver. Lock it in too soon, before culture shapes and battle hardens it, and it loses its value.

Like Cameron, culture judges each facet of Red Pill operations—immediately, decisively, and brutally. Culture battle hardens everything we do. Each hardening improves the Red Pill operator's awareness of culture until the operator learns to align with culture in such a way that they wield culture like David's sling and use its force to Red Pill advantage.

> "Culture battle hardens everything we do."

Don't leave anything to chance. If you play the blue pill game, the cards will be stacked against you with no way to win. Create your Red Pill organization or PMO the Red Pill way, with strategy and patience. It's the only way to come out with a truly Red Pill organization in the end, not matter what you call it.

Culture is a cruel mistress. However, those who survive her and align with her have a formidable weapon in their grasp. They can now use her ruthlessness to benefit the company as a whole and every Red Pill operator is involved.

Like in the, "We learned a lot" case study, that CEO thought he had control of the organization. But when the board wanted more effectiveness, that self-assured executive landed in the parking lot with scuffed elbows and stained knees, as a new culture was unleashed. Unleashed culture has one qualifier: effectiveness.

"Unleashed culture has one qualifier: effectiveness."

While it's not an easy task, unwinding a twisted company culture is possible. Here are some tactics that will make it easier:

1. Make Strategic Alignment the standard for incentives and rewards.

With Strategic Alignment as the standard for incentives and rewards, WIIFM biases naturally pivot toward Strategic Alignment, making effectiveness easier. In doing so, your Red Pill BKO or PMO becomes so intricately woven into the culture that no one can dismantle it. Get the WIIFM right, and you'll hold the thrust lever in your hand. With minimal pressure, the company will slowly pivot toward more and more effectiveness.

1. Use blue pill motivation for effectiveness as a bargaining chip.

With the right motivation, even stolid blue pill diehards will agree to Red Pill changes. With the confidence to own it and the ability to sell it, a Red Pill operator can effect change in the face of strong opposition. Then, following through to a successful outcome widens the door for even more Red Pill changes.

The Gift In The Battle

Throughout this entire book we have talked about the battle: taking off the gloves, fighting on the back lot, and blowing up the Omega. The Red Pill way involves struggle. You cannot be Red Pill without it. There are naturals, but like in any other profession, they are rare.

Change always challenges the *status quo,* and blue pill people love the *status quo.* Instead of rigid rules, the Red Pill seeks flow and adaptability. Instead of strict criteria, the Red Pill seeks effectiveness. Instead of blind reacting, the Red Pill seeks to understand culture. Challenging core beliefs creates tension and brings up powerful emotions. Stir up all of these in a conference room, and you've got a fight on your hands.

The battle is the gift. It's not a frustrating side effect. The battle is the juice, the place where Red Pill philosophy turns into rock solid reality.

Every skirmish reveals more about culture. Every hand-to-hand match reveals the blue pill walls. Every fight provides key information about the WIIFM of each person involved, about the value of the individual venture, and about the culture. Each skirmish hardens the Red Pill operator, teaching him and developing his street smarts.

"Each mission gives the operator more confidence to keep pushing forward."

Each mission gives the operator more confidence to keep pushing forward. Every failure spotlights a block in the organization. Every success opens a vein of gold, showing more opportunity to expand even more.

Best of all, this philosophical discussion becomes a deliberate and actionable initiative when we add precise measurements. We've identified more than 20 functions of the Red Pill organization and quantified them on a sliding scale. Instead of Al Braverman eyeing up his trainee and shouting directions, now we're taking everything into the laboratory, hooking up to electrodes, and measuring milliseconds in front of a green screen.

Chapter 9 Summary

- The secret ingredient is culture.
- Red Pill operatives know how to identify the walls and ride the flow patterns of culture.
- Culture controls everything. It has no pity on the weak and no patience for the incompetent.
- Individuals might be mowed down—from the janitor to the president of the board—but the company lives on. This is culture.
- Challenge culture, and you'll land on the curb before you know what hit you.
- Red Pill operators have cultural awareness, but blue pill operators never see culture.
- The Red Pill PMO is likely a blue pill trap! Ward off a blue pill coup by knowing it's coming and using it as a tool to strengthen your position.
- Culture designs the PMO piece by piece, not executives—regardless of whether they are Red Pill or blue pill.
- Unleashed culture has one qualifier: effectiveness.
- To unwind a twisted company culture:
  1. Make Strategic Alignment the standard for incentives and rewards.
  2. Use the thirst for effectiveness as a bargaining chip.

CHAPTER 10

Throw Out Your Old Yardstick

"There is nothing so useless as doing efficiently
that which should not be done at all."

~Peter Drucker[93]

What makes an operation successful? Until we understood what success looked like in practical terms, we couldn't measure it. We also couldn't track progress or plan for improvements.

When we started consulting in operations in 2003, we entered an industry with a massive 68% project fail rate that kept sliding downward. Why would a system with such a dismal record continue unchanged? Even then, over 16 years ago, we knew that something was missing. Something was off balance.

To find the solution, we kept asking that question and probing that idea: What makes operations initiatives successful?

We looked at the Triple Constraint Model and found the parameters of time, cost, and

"What makes
operations initiatives
successful?

scope/quality left out the critical component of Business Value. The very idea of discarding the Triple Constraints as the primary markers of success was so heretical, we used *The Matrix* as a metaphor and called our approach the Red Pill model. Our unshakable goal: to see the world as it really was, not as traditional wisdom said it was. We resolved to continue our quest until we had a definitive answer to our question.

From there, we determined that the true purpose of operations is adding value to the company.

We looked at the value of individual initiatives as the primary indicator for whether to move forward or not. If the benefit wasn't worth the cost, the plan came off the whiteboard. We advocated for free exchange of information from the board room to the conference room, so we could understand the true value equation and speak out whenever costs loomed larger than benefits—regardless of how far along the operation had progressed. Cancelling an initiative or project quickly was a win because it saved company resources.

Strategic Alignment was also a factor. Only initiatives in alignment with the company's purpose and goals were worth pursuing. We quickly learned maintaining alignment can be difficult because bias often compromises fidelity.

We turned to the human element and focused on improving our team. We studied brain science and identified key traits of high achievers. We trained our team using Limbic Learning and built a kick-butt group of operators. As a result, our stats started on the upward trend that continues to this day.

Still, we weren't satisfied. We knew we could do better. Something more was still missing.

Switching our primary focus to capturing maximum Business Value meant we had to soften the walls of the Iron Triangle. Time, cost, and scope must adjust when opportunities open up. The Red Pill executive stays alert for increasing value potential, then adjusts the scope and resources accordingly.

We developed the concept of the three-sided table and gave more ownership to project leaders. We taught them that increasing Business Value also increased their own effectiveness.

We passed out red pills to anyone within our client organizations who would take them. Those Red Pill operators began delivering more and more Business Value until they built a reputation for effectiveness. Over time, these operators coalesced into informal Red Pill Organizations that could eventually solidify into a formal department within their company.

This progression happened organically. It could not happen by mandate or training, because the Red Pill mindset means a fundamental shift in belief systems. Red Pill operators dig in and keep slugging when everything goes FUBAR. They show up after midnight, still wearing their tux from the night before and stay at the job until everything's cleaned up. They head out in a tried-and-true fishing boat to kill the Great White, and when they find out they need a bigger boat, they get a bigger boat.

This has to happen at the core level. Any operator who tries to fake it till they make it, will run like their tail's on fire when System 1 kicks in—and it always does. Any company who tries to mandate a Red Pill Organization will find it morphing back to blue pill almost immediately. Without a Red Pill heart, their team can't hold steady and true when the plane's engines fail and they are in the nose cone, first in line for impact.

However, once in place, the Red Pill Organization becomes an integral part of the company's effectiveness system that no one can dismantle.

We noticed effectiveness acting as a form of currency. Effective people carried weight that could alter the course of events within the company. They could make statements outside the norm and still be heard. They could go against tradition and still have a job… most of the time.

However, on occasion, even effectiveness currency wasn't enough. Push too hard and that person felt a recoil that could land them on the sidewalk, regardless if they were the Chairman of the Board or the CEO. One company we worked with fired its long-standing CEO despite great performance.

Why?

The question kept us stymied for years. If capturing more Business Value equals success, why would pushing for more success result in a backlash? When blue pill individuals block progress, we called that a blue wall. But that concept wasn't big enough. Something more held everything and everyone—Red Pill or blue pill—inside an invisible framework. We played blind man's bluff, reaching out until we felt resistance, stumbling around to get the lay of the land, straining to understand what we could sense but we could not see.

Over the course of 16 years, we slammed into this *glass boundary* and bruised our noses time and time again. We fell and scraped our knees. We made assumptions and got ourselves kicked to the curb.

Finally, we got it. That glass boundary was culture and every company has a unique one.

Red Pill operators develop a sensitivity to culture and learn to use it. Blue pill people resign themselves to culture and live within the world provided by others.

All those years, we had been dancing with culture without realizing it. Culture determines what happens, and what happens next. At a daily practical level, everything happens according to culture, not executive order or expensive methodologies.

Culture determines what success looks like. For some companies, it's growth. For others, success means a perfect record in customer service, or positive numbers at the bottom of a P/L sheet. For some, it's sales—regardless of tanking customer satisfaction or high team turnover rates due to impossible stress levels. The culture might be skewed or corrupted, dominant or subtle, but it's always the boss.

> "We had been dancing with culture for years without realizing it."

Each company has its own definition of success determined by its culture. That's why many operations and project management maturity models don't work in the real world. A study by the Project Management Institute confirms this:

We demonstrate that the maturity of project management implementations is a useful construct in understanding overall correlations of process capability with value, particularly as they related to the <u>consistency and formality of implemented practices.</u> However, we also show that maturity alone does not include an appreciation of the context within which practices are implemented, and that therefore any recommendations derived from maturity models, as they currently exist today must, of necessity, be suspect.[94] [Emphasis ours]

The Standard Maturity Model ignores culture in the attempt to create a one-size-fits-all answer using criteria that doesn't apply. No wonder project management statistics show the galloping fail rate of 70%.

This is why the Sydney Opera House could take 15 years to build, go over budget by 14 times and still be a massive success. The culture demanded distinctive architecture, excellent craftsmanship, and lavish detail. They wanted a masterpiece on a global scale, and they got it. Although important, how much it cost and how long it took came second to their primary standard of elegant presentation.

With culture as their blueprint, consultants and executives can shape their processes, their tools, their language, their staff, and every other aspect to align—not just with the strategy and mission—but to the culture as it exists in time. When they understand culture, they can ride the culture-current like it's the EAC and shout *Cowabunga!* as they arrive at their destination faster, better, and with more effectiveness than ever before.

The power of this concept rocked us back on our heels.

Derailed Purpose

By focusing on standardization and control, most traditional management training devolved into blindly following processes and staying within rigid parameters. This slowed down progress and sometimes derailed their objectives altogether. Over time, they forgot their original mission: moving the company forward.

Company culture defines success. Culture defines Strategic Alignment, Business Value related to dollars, Business Value not related to dollars, and the path to the future. When company leadership gets clear on these elements, decisions become intuitive and easy with a simple question: Will the benefit be worth the cost at this point in time?

"Decisions become intuitive and easy."

People form value-based judgments from System 1, their working model of the world. This same process can also happen at an organizational level. When company leaders become clear on cultural parameters, most questions will quickly bring up an intuitive answer, no analytics required.

Various levels within an organization naturally have different values. Culture flavors each of them. We call these distinctive viewpoints *bias*. For example, Operations often places high value on smooth procedures or pristine delivery. A project sponsor could value clear information, so they can make good decisions. Company leaders typically value Strategic Alignment to the company mission as well as overall profitability.

Some of these values have official standing as recorded goals, but others remain unwritten. Similar to Herzberg and Maslow's Hygiene Factor[95], culture tends to ignore things that don't stress it, and only focus on things that do. This is one of the reasons culture stays so invisible.

A New Yardstick

In our journey to quantify the many aspects of operations, standard assessment models failed us. They didn't address the variances within each cultural aquarium. They missed that organizations move like living organisms, each with its own view of the world. They missed that most companies are filled with blue pill operators focused on process and maturity instead of effectiveness. Their results didn't give us the information we needed.

To move forward, we had to create an interactive assessment to measure effectiveness. We called it the Think Effectiveness Assessment Model [TEAM][96] and Framework. We wanted to know how each function contributes, the degree it contributes, and how much time it would take to make it contribute more. We wanted to know how much blue wall resistance the company had and identify the open *culture-currents* we could use to our advantage. We needed to access the corporation's System 1, so we could identify the biases at each level of the company.

We taught ourselves to assess improvement and decline in more than 20 operational areas to draw a refined picture of progress. Never again would we ask, "How are things going?" to hear back, "Nothing is wrong here, especially near the nuclear reactor."

> "Effectiveness can only increase as the culture allows."

With this understanding of bias, resistance, and culture-currents, a new way of thinking about effectiveness and maturity emerged. Finally, we had a snapshot of the health of the living organism that is the company—almost like a medical MRI shows the body's existing state. Along with this insight came a healthy dose of respect.

Effectiveness can only increase as the culture allows. You can't take a hammer to the side of the aquarium and expect the fish to survive. When the glass cracks, everyone is in trouble. We can't emphasize it enough—treat cultural boundaries with care.

States of Culture

Looking over our own experience with past and present clients, we noticed several states of culture. There is a Natural State that has a *Lord of the Flies* rawness to it. Every group with a common purpose creates a unique culture within their community. They start out informal and unrestricted but, over time, they develop a framework of unwritten rules. Eventually they implement formal rules to create a feeling of safety and help the community reach some equilibrium. Culture in the Natural State is relatively stable unless acted upon by outside influences.

Culture goes into a more Constrained State when management brings in artificial mechanisms that tighten down control to force more productivity than the Natural State culture provides. In the event these controls disappear, the culture will mostly revert back to the Natural *Lord of the Flies* State.

In the Natural State and Constrained State, management has marginal awareness of culture's impact on effectiveness. Instinctively, they stay somewhat culturally aligned, so their staff accepts them as a given. With blue pill blindness, they simply work within the glass boundaries and don't think about them.

If leadership believes more control will force more productivity, they add more mechanisms. However, adding pressure also creates resistance in the ranks, an indicator that leadership might have blue pill blindness. People don't like change, especially when they feel hampered along with rising expectations for more output.

Also, during the hiring process, people buy into the company's mission and culture. If they feel pushed toward something outside that scope, they develop a vague sense of broken trust and could go into survival mode with behaviors that sabotage the intentions of leadership. This is where the glass can crack by applying too much pressure.

Sometimes easing the pressure means changing the senior team. Other times, that's not the best plan at all.

The goal is finding a way to dissolve resistance and open the flow of operations, like clearing a logjam on a river. With the block resolved, the culture-current will open up. However, before you set off dynamite to blow up a logjam, take careful stock of the situation. When you clear one logjam you might create several logjams further downriver. If upstream moves too fast, downstream soon becomes overwhelmed and might even shut down altogether.

"Find a way to dissolve resistance and open the flow of operations."

Logjams provide vital information by revealing points of resistance. In a jam, System 1 sounds off. Most operators slip into panic mode and autopilot into damage control. Going back to Limbic Learning, a System 1 response is your signal to pause and let System 2 come on-line. Explore the bigger picture. Deal with root causes. If you simply dynamite that curve in the river, it will cause all kinds of havoc downstream and block up again before too long.

The more you understand the cultural dynamics of your company, the easier you will predict downstream results with some degree of accuracy. Your Red Pill team will continually feed you critical information to keep the flow going at maximum velocity.

In a blue pill environment, too many logjams can destabilize the culture. If you are a Red Pill operative in a blue pill company, treat this with extreme care. Once team members reach a tipping point with frustration and confusion, everything could grind to a halt and you'll have to spend critical time making repairs.

Through this process, if you resolve your logjams and open the culture-currents, the next state of culture lies just ahead: Aspirational State.

In an Aspirational State, leadership realizes culture has nuclear power. These Red Pill leaders intentionally move the culture toward optimum effectiveness by strategically applying pressure—sometimes with intent and patience, and sometimes with a jolt. Knowing where the resistance lies, they can open the culture-current wider and wider for more effectiveness without a recoil.

In all these modifications and adjustments, one thing is constant. Culture moves slowly, but operations can change quickly. The only way to monitor culture's alignment to operations is to take regular snapshots and watch patterns appear.

The assessment process takes time. Talk to tacticians, managers, and executives in several passes. Understand how they determine, perceive, and measure effectiveness against their many functions—we interrogate more than 20 when we look at an organization. Uncover the unwritten rules. Figure out the pecking order. Stay alert for resistance and how to open culture-currents.

Watch how communications and activities flow, and you'll observe the blocks that slow them down. Some of these blocks are blue walls and some are cultural boundaries. Sometimes they are both. Blue walls come from localized agendas of blue pill people. Cultural boundaries are through and through. In some organizations, especially large ones, multiple cultures exist simultaneously, adding even more complexity.

Add your own specialized functions, like regulatory compliance, to the standard list of management and operational functions. Conduct artifact reviews to verify the reporting of your subjects.

Each pass of employee interaction peels back layers, so culture reveals itself. In the first pass, it's a simple journey of discovery. Anyone can see the obvious culture—the one the company wants you to see. *We're a sales-driven organization! Profitability for shareholders! We serve our community!* Companies strategically brand themselves as a certain type of culture. This is the skin on the onion. Keep peeling away layers to find out what's at the core.

Bias slows down operations and takes down effectiveness. Resistance and culture-currents form loops and whorls with the uniqueness of a fingerprint. Understanding your culture's fingerprint is where the power lies.

We're not going to sugar coat it. This assessment model is rigorous. If it seems easy, you're not doing it right. You must test your observations and judgments every step of the way, come at it from a different direction, and test again.

> "Understanding your culture's fingerprint is where the power lies."

In your company, what does culture actually measure as effective—as opposed to what the manual says is measures? What does the effectiveness equation leave out? Where are the biases?

Can you prove what you find? Which documents will provide compelling evidence? Over several passes and many interactions, the questions get tougher and tougher to bring out the truth and show the patterns.

Whatever assessment model you use, the process needs to have enough rigor to be valuable. Take a snapshot. Tweak. Take another snapshot. Tweak again.

Our TEAM Framework yields something similar to a mind map. It contains nodes that represent the operational functions with sub-categories under those nodes. Interconnecting lines show their relationships. We measure each node on a sliding scale from mature to immature, from critical to irrelevant, from culturally aligned to misaligned, and from effortless to labor intensive.

Once you have your results, you can put together an incremental performance plan to improve effectiveness. Take the plan one step at a time. Give the culture time to adjust before moving to the next phase.

Benefits of Culture-Currents and Resistance

Any culture will resist when asked to act outside its normal parameters. But what if you give a culture more of what it wants? Open culture-currents are where culture loves improvements. For example, in a culture that values loyalty and longevity in its employees, give that culture ways to increase loyalty and longevity and you'll be the company hero. Taking this idea one step further, if you can find a way to present any change as increasing loyalty and longevity, your initiative will have a much better chance of acceptance with no recoil.

Before you leap, however, double and triple check your plan against the bigger picture. Opening culture-currents to facilitate change in one area can create logjams in other areas of the business. For instance, one of our clients had a problem with accountability in their departments. Because their PM tool had a hefty accountability feature, they started using it for non-projects. Soon, portfolio management developed a logjam and ground to a halt. What seemed an easy solution created a crisis downriver.

Before you pull the trigger, examine the value of any resistance or open culture-currents. Does the culture truly value whatever you are measuring? Would culture rather

"Does the culture truly value whatever you are measuring?"

tolerate a situation instead of improve it? Notice visceral reactions during your interview process. We're after reality here. That's what the Red Pill is all about.

Going back to the distorted company that only valued sales, they pooh-poohed our observations about stress in customer service and the technical team because they had a high tolerance for those issues. They saw our recommendations for stress reduction as a waste of time and sent us packing. We missed seeing culture properly. Just because you see a slowdown doesn't mean the company will give you a gold star for solving that issue.

Taking another approach, you might deliberately open a culture-current in one area knowing you'll create a pile up elsewhere. Maybe that new logjam is next on your list of initiatives anyway, or maybe it will reveal resistance so you can resolve it. When you have a strategy, these discomforts have purpose. As part of the plan, your team's frustration at the inconvenience might be eased a little with less chance of recoil.

From a different angle, sometime a logjam has its root upstream. Instead of simply blasting away, you might want to check for causes and take action somewhere else instead. With this broader view of culture and how the organization operates within that culture, you can get past the WYSIATI mindset of looking at only what's immediately before you.

This is not a cut-and-dried science. Most people ignore it. They don't see or don't care that open culture-currents in one area might create logjams in others. A localized objective, coupled with selective blindness creates convoluted snags in the culture. Trying to make their own job easier, they make someone else's job harder. This also happens when someone applies a value across the board when it only matters in a localized area, such as policies for shift workers that carry over to administrative positions.

Left untended, fast-moving culture-currents that continually create logjams will eventually twist the culture into *knots* and hide what's really going on. If you're hearing cries for help within a certain sector or department, you've got a hot spot that needs a bigger view than simply prying a few logs loose and hoping that will do for now. Don't default to

System 1 when System 2 has to come on board for a complete resolution to the problem.

Deploying the Power of Culture

In this model, you can modify culture in a controlled setting. Whether you take the slow-and-steady route or blast away, this type of change is only for those committed to staying in the game when everything goes FUBAR—sort of like taking the red pill, by the way.

Sixteen years ago, at the beginning of our journey, our bare knuckled Red Pill style taught us to spot open culture-currents at a limbic subconscious level. Through trial and error and dead reckoning, we felt our way along and found what worked. We learned to rinse and repeat.

Moving forward with bigger and bigger accounts, this kind of seat-of-the-pants navigation became more challenging. A PMO could have hundreds of open projects with all sorts of blue pill eddies, bias undercurrents, and knotted culture.

Trying to implement a cultural shift over a twisted organization is like yanking the end of a knotted line. It only makes things worse. Before you begin, consider how you might untangle the culture one knot at a time. An old fisherman's secret to untangling a line is to use a light touch and work on the biggest loops first. Reframe the tangle as an opportunity, find your big loops and gently work at them.

Examine the business and the culture from the various levels and perspectives. Check out the areas of resistance and open culture-currents. Ask what this culture will allow. Test the boundaries. Find out how to resolve resistance and open more culture-currents. Tweak, then test and retest. Over our 16 years in business, this process of intentional change has opened most of the logjams that spurred our clients to call us.

A company spends years, often decades, hiring people who fit into their culture. Shifting those individuals to a new framework comes with challenges. This is one reason companies who make the choice to cross into No Man's Land usually crash. Transforming a smaller company to a major corporation involves cultural changes that the original team probably won't like, and hiring new people takes too long.

Three Approaches to Dealing with Cultural Change

In Chapter 2, Dan McCarthy's article "The Common Traits of Successful Senior Executives"[97] showed how leadership naturally pushes the company forward. Typical executives are dedicated to continuous improvement. When they decide where they want to go, they expect solutions and hate whining. They are risk takers and don't mind making mistakes. They move quickly and have short attention spans.

All of these are advantages in the areas of operations and leadership, but those traits will get an executive into trouble when it comes to cultural change. This process is counterintuitive—one reason for the high fail rate and why it's so difficult to turn that trend around.

Each company is unique, yes, but each department and level are also unique. A corporation is a multi-dimensional organism. What works in one area will wreak havoc in another. Take time to assess and choose carefully which of these options will work best for you:

1. More Change Faster
2. Less Change Slower But With Persistence
3. Violent, Rapid Change

1. More Change Faster

Case Study: Research Campus

Although a private corporation, this research campus had the culture of a slow-moving government agency where the majority of its 500 employees had been there forever. Like the stone structures on its grounds, the research campus had been around for a long time and will continue to be around for long time.

Their new director, we'll call him Ron, came onboard to bring more control and discipline to the organization through accountability.

Confident and charismatic, Ron had worked in several corporations before with great success. This is what he did, and why he landed the job.

Things went well at first, but before long Ron hit a barrier. His next steps wouldn't stick no matter what he tried. Things were getting worse instead of better, but he had an idea why. That's when he called us to implement our TEAM Framework.

After interviewing employees at all levels, we found resistance everywhere. The staff had steadily and softly undermined progress. They were hardwired into the culture of loose governance and lax accountability, and they couldn't conceive of such a change. As a result, the culture recoiled. Chaos grew by the day. *Lord of the Flies* was on its way.

Ron's options:

- More Change Faster. With resistance already on the rise, the staff had braced against the notion of still more changes. In fact, the current changes were under constant pressure to revert back to their original lax position.

- Less Change Slower But With Persistence. Although leadership wanted more control, they continued hiring employees who loved the loose accountability structure. Slow persistence was already the natural course of things.

- Violent, Rapid Change. Not here. No one had any appetite for the pain that comes from rapid, extreme change.

The Solution: Less Change Slower But With Persistence.

Retraining 500 people is like turning the Queen Mary. It takes a long time and a lot of determination. In a company that would only respond to slow change, the process could take years, including onboarding new hires to expect a more controlled culture. But others in management were steeped in and enabled the existing culture, even though Ron was tasked to bring more control.

"Pushing for changes beyond cultural tolerance would have been a major mistake."

The Less Change Slower method is the least effective because the culture will revert back if leadership gets tired or distracted away from long-term persistence. Even so, the slow method was the best choice for the research campus. Pushing for changes beyond cultural tolerance would have been a major mistake.

Strong leaders naturally want to push harder. If Ron had followed his usual inclination without looking deeper, more and more twists would have formed into hard knots. The company would have wasted more and more resources. As it was, they suffered a real setback from this effort because mounting confusion and frustration destabilized an organization whose foundational characteristic was stability.

Ron saved the company from greater pain because he paused for self-reflection.

Bringing about consistent change was Ron's purpose in the organization. He didn't have the personality or the desire to wait years for that to happen. After studying the assessment report, Ron realized his expertise and experience worked best in a culture that matched his More Change Faster approach—a major shift in his perspective of his own career. As a result, Ron left the research campus to seek a position with a culture more suited to his workstyle.

Overall, the company did see some lasting improvement in accountability. They also learned more about their culture. Saving the company's resources was also a win but reining them in before they shattered their glass boundary was priceless.

2. Less Change Slower But With Persistence

Case Study: Green Tech Company

This fast-tech company had a culture rooted in loose control and spotty accountability. About 75% of their employees were young, energetic technicians who loved the think tanks, the creative juice, and the aliveness of the open workspace. However, the company's structure allowed for overlapping roles and divided loyalties. Sectors of the business had split into possessive, self-protective subcultures and silos. Suspicion, gossip, and open conflict had become part of their daily lives.

> "Without a definite plan, they ended up knotting their own culture."

Leadership had tried Less Change Slower several times but failed because they lacked patience and persistence. Without a definite plan and the desire to stick to it, they made change for the sake of change inconsistently, and ended up knotting their own rope.

Leadership was ready to make a full out commitment to follow through. They knew it was time to end the chest-thumping and redirect that energy into expanding their most profitable ventures.

Their options:

- More Change Faster. To see lasting change, leadership had to slow down. Although the team had an open attitude toward adjustments, leadership lacked persistence. Without follow through, the culture always reverted back. In this case, fast thinking and fast moving was part of their problem.

- Less Change Slower But With Persistence. They didn't have time to wait. Leadership felt intense pressure to solve this long-term problem once and for all. Also, cultural resistance would be relatively low because their team liked seat-of-the-pants navigation. On the flip side of that coin, however, their fast pace made all change seem temporary, and they didn't take it too seriously. Positioned as a permanent solution to open a culture-current, the team would better align with this modification.

- Violent, Rapid Change. Leadership had already taken some steps, and the team had responded with relief, not disruption. This was a positive sign that a jolt wouldn't be necessary. With their new cultural awareness and substantial resources, they could take intense, persistent action and achieve their goal without taking the stress level to that point.

The Solution: Take intense measures but stop short of a jolt.

As the silos dissolved, they pointed out the open culture-currents as a reward for preserving this change. They sold their team on a unified vision and set up a regular routine to check in and course-correct. They also started hiring a different type of people at middle level and tasked them with enforcing persistence.

As it turned out, this company made an operational change, not a true cultural change. They are still the same young, smart, energetic business, just a tighter ship with more vision. And that's okay. Their effectiveness has reached new levels and continues to climb.

3. Violent, Rapid Change

Case Study: Epilogue to "We Learned a Lot"

Developing eco-friendly, green products, this company achieved such success after their shift to the Red Pill. They decided to cross into No Man's Land and head for the big time. Their highly creative team was deeply vested in company culture. Many of them worked remotely three days a week, brought their pets to work, and enjoyed on-site daycare when they did come to the office. These employees saw the organization as doing good in the world. Everyone was emotionally bonded to the value-driven mission.

After firing their CEO, they brought us in to establish control and help them in their new expansion. Led by highly entrepreneurial and ego-driven leadership (nothing wrong with that), the culture typically accepted rapid change.

Their objective: to leap across No Man's Land in a very short period of time.

In this case, the board had already chosen Violent, Abrupt Change, perhaps without full awareness of the massive energy in resources and dogged determination this option would require. They delivered an ultimatum to their employees—adapt-or-leave—and some left.

This is an ongoing story with pain as the central theme. The result will be a completely new culture. Their new leadership has a financially driven mission, so the new culture no longer matches their original emotionally bonded employees.

We can look at this situation in two ways. Our experience tells us the disruption and pain inflicted on the business wasn't entirely necessary. This jolt left a trail of wreckage that continues to play out as more and more of their original employees find better suited positions elsewhere.

With better cultural awareness and use of the TEAM Framework they could have made a smoother transition. However, maybe smooth and simple wasn't important to them. Maybe they just wanted to get it done. In that case, this scenario would be a win.

Not A Quick Fix

Opening culture-currents doesn't happen overnight. Each company must cover the territory to reach its destination, the same as taking a trip from Baltimore to Seattle. You might have a GPS, but you'll still have to cross the country to get there.

Every stage of the journey is important. Overzealous Red Pill recruits often want to jump ahead with hardline tactics and a forcing attitude. They usually end up creating a disaster both personally and for the company. Jumping ahead too quickly can diminish effectiveness.

In the movie, *Edge of Tomorrow*, this concept plays out in an interesting way. The armies of Earth had a culture of WYSIATI. They had sacrificed thousands of lives already and kept sending more soldiers to certain death. Their strategy was ineffective, but they kept on just the same.

Culture said the way to win was to keep pushing forward and overwhelm the enemy in front of them. However, the real enemy lay hidden in a dark recess deep underwater. Killing mimics would never win the war.

In the movie, the General represents culture. Eventually, Cage determines he must confront the General to get a device that would give them the location of the Omega. However, convincing culture to do things a different way isn't easy. We don't know how many attempts Cage and Rita made. First, they had to reach the General's office, then convince him to turn over the device and, finally, to escape the building without ending up in jail.

That one scenario took dozens, if not hundreds, of attempts, but the journey didn't start there. The journey began when Cage realized he had to do things a different way. He saw no way of surviving on the beach and took a different track. He found someone to show him a different perspective and took the training he needed. He perfected his fighting skills and connected with his warrior's heart.

One step at a time, he made his way closer and closer to his goal: taking out the Omega. When he finally made it to the General's office he said, "I'm going to tell you a story, General. At first it will sound ridiculous, but the longer I talk the more rational it's going to appear."

Isn't that the conversation of everyone who confronts culture? At first, they see your viewpoint as ridiculous, but over time your Red Pill thinking begins to make more sense.

One step at a time, with patience and commitment, you will reach your destination if you keep going and don't give up.

First, take off the rose-colored glasses where "Everything is fine here. Especially near the nuclear reactor," and answer these questions. What does effectiveness mean in your culture and how effective is your team? Are your operations initiatives producing Business Value in the real world?

Then take a good look in the mirror:

Are you a Red Pill operator who sees the world as it really is?

Are you willing to take off the gloves and go to the back lot when stuff gets real?

Are you ready to speak out for open information exchange in the conference room?

Are you committed to Strategic Alignment to the company's mission and culture?

Do you have the *cojones* to kill a project the moment the cost outweighs the benefits?

Once you are clear on these points, your next step is to improve yourself and your team. Find your high achievers and train them using Limbic Learning. Build a kick-butt group of operators; make effectiveness instinctual. Give them coaching and tools to keep them sharp. Show them how to open culture-currents and how to ride those currents to success. Reframe logjams and blue walls as vital information for your arsenal.

Bring the three-sided table into your process and allow, no insist, that project leaders take ownership. Reward them for capturing maximum Business Value. Soften the walls of the Iron Triangle so the time, cost and scope can adjust as opportunities open up.

When your heroes rise to the top, encourage them to work together. Watch them coalesce into an informal Red Pill Organization without trying to structure them or restrict them. Let the process happen organically as trust and respect develops between them. Create a nourishing environment where they can test their mettle and harden to the fight.

While your Red Pill Organization develops, put together your own stash of Effectiveness Benjamins, so you can negotiate for even more effectiveness. Earn your right to make bold statements that will be heard. Test the boundaries of culture systematically and persistently. Study your company's fingerprint until you know every loop and whorl.

If and when your company grows to the point of No Man's Land, take advantage of the opportunity to aim the culture toward more effectiveness. Build a solid staircase to success one riser at a time. That's the journey of the Red Pill warrior.

What If You Knew You Couldn't Lose?

If you knew you couldn't lose, how confident would you feel? How easy would it be to take ownership? How motivated would you be to hang in there when everything goes sideways?

You have the ultimate cheat code in your hands right now. No more guessing or fighting blind. You have the progression from start to finish.

It's time to make a solid commitment to get this done. Put together a kick-butt crew and go further than anyone has ever gone before. Fill your pockets with Effectiveness Benjamins.

And, for goodness sake, land the plane.

Chapter 10 Summary

- Every company has a glass boundary called culture.
- Operators who understand culture can ride the culture-current and arrive at their destination faster, better and with more effectiveness than ever before.
- Culture flavors the various levels within an organization. We call this bias.
- Our interactive assessment called the Think Effectiveness Assessment Model [TEAM] Framework gives us a snapshot of a company's culture.
- From our observations, the three states of culture are Natural, Constrained, and Aspirational.
- This rigorous assessment process takes time.
  - » Interview people at every level.
  - » Add your own specialized functions to the standard list of management functions.
  - » Conduct artifact reviews to verify the reporting of your subjects.
  - » Understand your culture's fingerprint is where the power lies.
  - » Take a snapshot. Tweak. Take another snapshot. Tweak again.
  - » Put together an incremental performance plan to improve effectiveness.
- To ride the culture-currents, give the culture more of what it wants.
- Logjams will eventually twist the culture into knots and hide what's really going on.
- In a controlled setting, you can modify culture, but this isn't a quick fix.
- Always proceed with caution.

ABOUT THE AUTHORS

Jeff Welch, Bryan Wolbert, and Tony Gruebl

Jeff Welch, Bryan Wolbert, and Tony Gruebl are principles of Think Systems, Inc., (simply called, Think) a seventeen-year-old operations consulting firm headquartered in Baltimore, Maryland. Together, the authors have over seventy-five years of experience in Operations, Technology, Finance, and Learning & Development.

Tony is Think's President and a former COO and VP in the software industry. Jeff is an engineer by trade, an Agile Transformation Coach, and he has worked as a lead Learning Solution Architect for Pearson Performance, Vangent, and later PDRI. Bryan is the current COO of Think and leader of Think's Strategic Hiring division, and is a former lead business analyst/project manager for T. Rowe Price and later Merkle, Inc.

Their first book, *Bare Knuckled Project Management (BKPM): How to Succeed at Every Project,* by Tony Gruebl and Jeff Welch, has more than 15,000 copies in circulation and is available as an audiobook.

Visit Think's web site at http://www.thinksi.com

GLOSSARY

Please Note: The first time these terms appear within the text, they are italicized.

Adaptive: flexible parameters that capture the most Business Value Potential possible

Aspirational State: ease of flow via open culture-currents

Bare Knuckled Organization: spontaneous group of Red Pill operatives who work together to create value and improve effectiveness

Bias: an individual's perspective on what is valuable and what is not valuable

Business Value Potential: the maximum benefit a project can capture

Causal Reasoners: improvisers who develop goals on the fly while creatively reacting to contingencies

Cognitive Frame Switching: considering a situation from several perspectives

Constrained State: culture under pressure as management tightens control to force productivity

Culture-current: a smooth flow in operations that adds momentum to a project

Eddies: similar to swirling water, operations in a spin without forward motion

Effectual Reasoners: systematic, logical thinkers who set a goal and create steps to reach it

Fidelity: staying aligned with an honest and true account

Growth through cellular division: the natural spread of Red Pill thinking as people work together

Glass boundary: cultural parameters, the dividing line between what is acceptable and what is unacceptable

Intentional Instinct: pre-planned responses based on Limbic Learning

Kickoff Readiness Process: system that prepares an initiative for launch

Knots: the hidden blocks in a convoluted or skewed culture

Logjam: stalled workflow due to overwhelm, confusion, and resistance

Natural State: culture in the raw, elemental state similar to *Lord of the Flies*

Neuroplasticity: the ability of the brain to form new synaptic connections, especially in response to learning or experience

Project: set of coordinated and controlled activities to capture or retain the most value possible from a larger value potential

Rapid Control Process: quickly taking charge of a project in crisis

Red Pill Evolution: morphing a blue pill organization into a Red Pill organization

Resting Zone: natural state or comfort zone

Role Shifting: switching from strategic to tactical thinking and back again

Silo: a company sub-culture with a protective attitude toward their territory

SRO: Strategy Realization Office

Strategic Information Provisioning: delivering specific wisdom at particular intervals, sometimes called coaching or mentoring

Three-Sided Table: the Red Pill model for project management where the sponsor, project manager, and technical team each work from their own side of a triangular table

RESOURCES

"Abilene Paradox, DR. HARVEY, 1981." YouTube.com: 23 July 2016, Video. Accessed 27 June 2018. https://www.youtube.com/watch?v=uFQ-ukyvAMks

"The Abilene Paradox." Communication Videos: A CRM Release. Media-Partners.com: Accessed 27 June 2018. http://www.abileneparadox.com

Bloch, Michael et.al. "Delivering Large-Scale IT Projects On Time, On Budget, And On Value." McKinsey & Company: Digital McKinsey, October 2012. https://www.mckinsey.com/business-functions/digital-mckinsey/our-insights/delivering-large-scale-it-projects-on-time-on-budget-and-on-value

Bonnie, Emily. "Complete Collection of Project Management Statistics 2015." Wrike.com: 7 July 2015, Accessed 15 September 2017.

Buchanan, Leigh "How Great Entrepreneurs Think." Inc.com: 1 February 2011, Accessed 27 June 2018. https://www.inc.com/magazine/20110201/how-great-entrepreneurs-think.html

Chuck, Millennium Films. IMDb.com: 5 May 2017, http://www.imdb.com/title/tt1610525/.

Crawford, J. Kent. *The Strategic Planning Office: A Guide to Improving Organizational Performance.* New York: Marcel Dekker, Inc., 2002.

DiNapoli, Tom. "Classic Movie Line #22." YouTube.com, 13 February 2008. Accessed June 27, 2018. https://www.youtube.com/watch?v=jh-dhGlsh98

Dobson, M. S. and Heidi Feickert. *The Six Dimensions of Project Management* Oakland, CA: Berrett-Koehler Publishers, 2007.

Dowling, Kyle. "Surviving Disasters in Project Management: An Interview with Dr. Harold Kerzner." The Huffington Post: 13 January 2014, Accessed 27 June 2018. http://www.huffingtonpost.com/kyle-dowling/surviving-disasters-in-pr_b_4590442.html

"East Australian Current." Wikipedia: Accessed 4 December 2018. https://en.wikipedia.org/wiki/East_Australian_Current

Edge of Tomorrow. Warner Bros Pictures: 2014. http://www.imdb.com/title/tt1631867/?ref_=nv_sr_1

Flyvbjerg, Bent and Alexander Budzier. "Why Your IT Project May Be Riskier Than You Think." HBR.org: Harvard Business Review, September 2011.

Frese, Robert and Dr. Vicki Sauter. "Project Success and Failure: What Is Success, What Is Failure, And How Can You Improve Your Odds For Success?" University of Missouri-St. Louis: 16 December 2003, Accessed 27 June 2018. http://www.umsl.edu/~sauterv/analysis/6840_f03_papers/frese/

Gaybutton. "Wrong." YouTube.com: 15 January 2012. Accessed June 27, 2018. https://www.youtube.com/watch?v=AJLqTYAhlgk

Gruebl, Tony. "5 Strategies for Delivering Bad News: Roseanne Roseannadanna, tell them the truth!" LinkedIn.com, 17 July 2017. https://www.linkedin.com/pulse/5-strategies-delivering-bad-news-roseanne-tell-them-tony-gruebl/

Gruebl, Tony, Jeff Welch, et al. *Bare Knuckled Project Management: How to Succeed at Every Project.* Baltimore: Gameplan Press, 2013.

Gruebl, Tony and Jeff Welch. "Triple Constraint Theory Fails in the Field." *PM Magazine.* Baltimore: Morgan State University, Spring 2016. https://issuu.com/morganstate/docs/msu_pmmagazine_spring2016_r4?e=23887085/36536018

Haner, James L. "Recipe for Project Success: The CHAOS Top Ten." Learning Tree® International: 27 September 2013, Accessed 28 June 28, 2018. https://blog.learningtree.com/recipe-for-project-success-the-chaos-top-ten/

Halt and Catch Fire. TV Series. AMC Studios: 2014-2017. https://www.imdb.com/title/tt2543312/?ref_=ttpl_pl_tt

Jaws. Zanuck/Brown Productions. IMDB.com: 20 June 1975. http://www.imdb.com/title/tt0073195/?ref_=nv_sr_1

Johnson, Jim interviews Ken Schwaber. "PM Agile Role" Episode #103. CHAOS Tuesday Podcast: 15 December 2015, Accessed 27 June 2018. http://www.chaostuesday.com/index.php?r=podcast/view&id=105

Kahneman, Daniel. *Thinking, Fast and Slow*, 1st paperback ed. New York: Farrar, Straus and Giroux, 2013.

McCarthy, Dan. "The Common Traits of Successful Senior Executives." The Balance.com: 28 August 2017, Accessed 27 June 2018. https://www.thebalance.com/characteristics-of-most-successful-senior-executives-2275904

The Matrix, Warner Bros Pictures. IMDb.com: 31 March 1999.

"The Matrix" Wikipedia.org: Accessed 27 June 2018. https://en.wikipedia.org/wiki/The_Matrix#Development

McChesney, Chris, Sean Covey and Jim Huling. *The 4 Disciplines of Execution*, 2nd edition. New York: Free Press, 12 April 2016.

Mullaly, M. E. & J. Thomas. "Re-thinking project management maturity: perspectives gained from explorations of fit and value." Paper presented at PMI® Research Conference: Defining the Future of Project Management. Washington, DC., Newtown Square, PA: Project Management Institute, 2010. https://www.pmi.org/learning/library/management-maturity-model-performance-assessment-6491

Needs, Ian. "Why PMOs Fail: 5 Shocking PMO Statistics." KeyedIN.com: Accessed 1 November 2018. https://www.keyedin.com/keyedinprojects/article/why-pmos-fail-5-shocking-pmo-statistics/

Nelson, J. K., S. J. Zaccaro, and J. L. Herman. "Strategic information provision and experiential variety as tools for developing adaptive leadership skills." *Consulting Psychology Journal: Practice and Research,* 62(2). APAPsychNet.com: 2010. http://psycnet.apa.org/record/2010-13314-006

Peterson, Jordan. *12 Rules for Life: An Antidote to Chaos.* Ontario: Random House Canada, 23 January 2018.

Pettey, Christy, contributor. "Don't Leave the PPM Strategy to Chance." Gartner, Inc.: 9 March 2017. http://www.gartner.com/smarterwithgartner/dont-leave-the-ppm-strategy-to-chance

"PMI's Pulse of the Profession: Capturing the Value of Project Management." PMI.org/Pulse: Project Management Institute, February 2015. http://www.pmi.org/-/media/pmi/documents/public/pdf/learning/thought-leadership/pulse/pulse-of-the-profession-2015.pdf

"PMI's Pulse of the Profession: The High Cost of Low Performance." PMI.org/Pulse: Project Management Institute: February 2014. http://www.pmi.org/-/media/pmi/documents/public/pdf/learning/thought-leadership/pulse/pulse-of-the-profession-2014.pdf

Pulp Fiction. Miramax. IMDb.com: 14 December 1994, http://www.imdb.com/title/tt0110912/?ref_=ttfc_fc_tt

Rocky, Chartoff-Winkler Productions. IMDb.com: 3 December 1976. http://www.imdb.com/title/tt0075148

Schurenberg, Eric. "Nobel Laureate Daniel Kahneman on Making Smarter Decisions." Podcast. Inc.com: Accessed 28 June 28, 2018. www.inc.com/daniel-kahneman/idea-lab-making-smarter-decisions.html

"The State of the PMO 2016: Enabling Strategy Execution Excellence." PMSolutions.com: 2016, Accessed 27 June 2018. http://www.pmsolutions.com/reports/State_of_the_PMO_2016_Research_Report.pdf

"The State of the PMO 2010: A PM Solutions Research Report." PMSolutions.com: 2010, Accessed 27 June 2018. http://www.

pmsolutions.com/collateral/research/State%20of%20the%20
PMO%202010%20Research%20Report.pdf

Sully Warner Bros Pictures. IMDb.com: 9 September 2016. http://www.
imdb.com/title/tt3263904/

"Take Your Worst Estimate and Double It: Project Management for
Postdocs." ScienceMag.org: March 15, 2002. http://www.
sciencemag.org/careers/2002/03/take-your-worst-estimate-and-
double-it-project-management-postdocs

Tatum, Doug. *No Man's Land: Where Growing Companies Fail*, reprint
edition. New York: Portfolio, 30 December 2008.

This Day in History. "Nuclear disaster at Chernobyl." History.com: 26
April 1986. http://www.history.com/this-day-in-history/nuclear-
disaster-at-chernobyl

"Two-factor theory." Wikipedia: Accessed 4 December 2018. https://
en.wikipedia.org/wiki/Two-factor_theory

Tzu, Sun, translated by Lionel Giles. *The Art of War*. BrainyQuote.com,
Accessed June 28, 2018. https://www.brainyquote.com/quotes/
sun_tzu_387509

Velayudhan, Divya P. and Dr. Sam Thomas. *The International Journal of
Business & Management*, Volume 4, Issue 4. Ontario: Canadian
Center of Science and Education, April 2016. http://www.
theijbm.com/wp-content/uploads/2016/04/6.-BM1604-014.pdf

Welch, Jeff. "Executive Project Expectations… is failure baked-in?"
ThinkSI.com: 1 February, 2016, Accessed 27 June 2018. https://
thinksi.com/2016/02/executive-project-expectations-is-failure-
baked-in-2/

Welch, Jeffrey S., *BKPM Pocket Guide: For Project Managers*. CreateSpace
Independent Publishing Platform: 20 March 2015.

"Why Up to 75% of Software Projects Will Fail." Geneca.com, 25 January
2017.

Wyngaard, C.J., et al. "Theory of the Triple Constraint – a Conceptual
Review." *Industrial Engineering and Engineering Management*.
ResearchGate.net: 2012, Accessed 27 June 2018. https://www.

researchgate.net/publication/271455172_Theory_of_the_triple_
constraint_-_A_conceptual_review

ENDNOTES

1   Divya P. Velayudhan and Dr. Sam Thomas, *The International Journal of Business & Management,* Volume 4, Issue 4 (Ontario: Canadian Center of Science and Education, April 2016), 48. http://www.theijbm.com/wp-content/uploads/2016/04/6.-BM1604-014.pdf

2   *The Matrix*, Warner Bros Pictures, IMDb.com, 31 March 1999. http://www.imdb.com/title/tt0133093/?ref_=nv_sr_1

3   Divya P. Velayudhan and Dr. Sam Thomas, *The International Journal of Business & Management.*

4   Michael Bloch, et.al, "Delivering Large-Scale IT Projects On Time, On Budget, And On Value," (Web: McKinsey & Company: Digital McKinsey, October 2012). https://www.mckinsey.com/business-functions/digital-mckinsey/our-insights/delivering-large-scale-it-projects-on-time-on-budget-and-on-value

5   "Why Up to 75% of Software Projects Will Fail," (Web: Geneca.com, 25 January 2017).

6   Bent Flyvbjerg and Alexander Budzier, "Why Your IT Project May Be Riskier Than You Think," (HBR.org: *Harvard Business Review*, September 2011).

7   "PMI's Pulse of the Profession: Capturing the Value of Project Management," (PMI.org/Pulse: Project Management Institute, February 2015), 3. http://www.pmi.org/-/media/pmi/documents/public/pdf/learning/thought-leadership/pulse/pulse-of-the-profession-2015.pdf

8   Divya P. Velayudhan and Dr. Sam Thomas, *The International Journal of Business & Management.*

9   The Standish Group, Project Resolution Benchmark for IBEX Finan-

cial Corp, May 16, 2018. https://www.standishgroup.com/sample_research_files/DemoPRBR.pdf

10   *Jaws*, Zanuck/Brown Productions, 20 June 1975. http://www.imdb.com/title/tt0073195/?ref_=nv_sr_1

11   Ibid.

12   This Day in History: "Nuclear disaster at Chernobyl," (Web: History.com, 26 April 1986). http://www.history.com/this-day-in-history/nuclear-disaster-at-chernobyl

13   Tony Gruebl, "5 Strategies for Delivering Bad News: Roseanne Roseannadanna, tell them the truth!" (Web: LinkedIn.com, 17 July 2017). https://www.linkedin.com/pulse/5-strategies-delivering-bad-news-roseanne-tell-them-tony-gruebl/

14   Jeff Welch, "Executive Project Expectations… is failure baked-in?" (Web: ThinkSI.com, 1 February, 2016, Accessed 27 June 2018) https://thinksi.com/2016/02/executive-project-expectations-is-failure-baked-in-2/

15   Divya P. Velayudhan and Dr. Sam Thomas, *The International Journal of Business & Management.*

16   "Take Your Worst Estimate and Double It: Project Management for Postdocs," ScienceMag.org, March 15, 2002. http://www.sciencemag.org/careers/2002/03/take-your-worst-estimate-and-double-it-project-management-postdocs

17   "The State of the PMO 2016: Enabling Strategy Execution Excellence,"(Web: PMSolutions.com, 2016, Accessed 27 June 2018). http://www.pmsolutions.com/reports/State_of_the_PMO_2016_Research_Report.pdf

18   Ibid.

19   Divya P. Velayudhan and Dr. Sam Thomas. *The International Journal of Business & Management*, 49.

20   "The State of the PMO 2016: Enabling Strategy Execution Excellence."

21   Divya P. Velayudhan and Dr. Sam Thomas. *The International Journal of Business & Management*, 49.

22   "The State of the PMO 2010: A PM Solutions Research Report," (Web: PMSolutions.com, 2010, Accessed 27 June 2018). http://www.pmsolutions.com/collateral/research/State%20of%20the%20PMO%202010%20Research%20Report.pdf

23   Ibid.

24   *Edge of Tomorrow*, Warner Bros Pictures (2014). http://www.imdb.com/title/tt1631867/?ref_=nv_sr_1

25   Ibid.

26   Author Unknown, (Web: Quora.com, 11 May 2017, Accessed 27 June 2018). https://www.quora.com/Did-Einstein-really-define-insanity-as-doing-the-same-thing-over-and-over-again-and-expecting-different-results

27   Robert Frese and Dr. Vicki Sauter, "Project Success and Failure: What Is Success, What Is Failure, And How Can You Improve Your Odds For Success?" (Web: University of Missouri-St. Louis, 16 December 2003, Accessed 27 June 2018). http://www.umsl.edu/~sauterv/analysis/6840_f03_papers/frese/

28   Kyle Dowling, "Surviving Disasters in Project Management: An Interview with Dr. Harold Kerzner," (Web: The Huffington Post, 13 January 2014, Accessed 27 June 2018). http://www.huffingtonpost.com/kyle-dowling/surviving-disasters-in-pr_b_4590442.html

29   Dr. Kerzner's books include: *Project Management: A Systems Approach to Planning, Scheduling and Controlling* (in its ninth edition as of this writing), *In Search of Excellence in Project Management, Applied Project Management and Strategic Planning for Project Management Using a Project Management Maturity Model*, and *Project Management Best Practices: Achieving Global Excellence*. You can find him on LinkedIn at https://www.linkedin.com/in/drharoldkerzner/.

30   James L. Haner, "Recipe for Project Success: The CHAOS Top Ten," (Web: Learning Tree* International, 27 September 2013, Accessed 28 June 28, 2018). https://blog.learningtree.com/recipe-for-project-success-the-chaos-top-ten/

31   *Edge of Tomorrow.* http://www.imdb.com/title/tt1631867/?ref_=nv_sr_1

32   Tony Gruebl and Jeff Welch, "Triple Constraint Theory Fails in the Field," *PM Magazine*, (Baltimore: Morgan State University, Spring 2016), 5-6. https://issuu.com/morganstate/docs/msu_pmmagazine_spring2016_r4?e=23887085/36536018

33   Gaybutton, "Wrong." https://www.youtube.com/watch?v=AJLqTYAhlgk

34   C.J. Wyngaard, et al, "Theory of the Triple Constraint – a Conceptual

Review" Industrial Engineering and Engineering Management (Web: Research-Gate.net, 2012, Accessed 27 June 2018), 1991-1997. https://www.researchgate.net/publication/271455172_Theory_of_the_triple_constraint_-_A_conceptual_review

35   M. S. Dobson and Heidi Feickert, *The Six Dimensions of Project Management,* (Oakland, CA: Berrett-Koehler Publishers, 2007).

36   Tony Gruebl, Jeff Welch, et al, *Bare Knuckled Project Management: How to Succeed at Every Project*, (Baltimore: Gameplan Press, 2013). https://www.amazon.com/Bare-Knuckled-Project-Management-Succeed/dp/0615813941)

37   Email from M. S. Dobson to Tony Gruebl, March 14, 2016, used with permission.

38   Ibid.

39   *Edge of Tomorrow.* http://www.imdb.com/title/tt1631867/?ref_=nv_sr_1

40   "The humans" is the way that John Hill, former VP of Think Systems, Inc., referred to the most uncontrollable variable in all activities and interactions with your client. This phrase is used in homage to Mr. Hill.

41   Jim Johnson interviews Ken Schwaber, "PM Agile Role" Episode #103, (Web: CHAOS Tuesday Podcast, 15 December 2015, Accessed 27 June 2018). http://www.chaostuesday.com/index.php?r=podcast/view&id=105

42   Dan McCarthy, "The Common Traits of Successful Senior Executives," (Web: The Balance.com, 28 August 2017, Accessed 27 June 2018). https://www.thebalance.com/characteristics-of-most-successful-senior-executives-2275904

43   Ibid.

44   Email from Dan McCarthy to Tony Goebl, July 14, 2017, used with permission.

45   Ja. A, "Abilene Paradox, DR. HARVEY, 1981," YouTube.com, 23 July 2016, Video. Accessed 27 June 2018. https://www.youtube.com/watch?v=uFQ-ukyvAMk

46   "The Abilene Paradox," Communication Videos: A CRM Release. Media-Partners.com. Accessed 27 June 2018. http://www.abileneparadox.com

47   Chris McChesney, Sean Covey and Jim Huling, *The 4 Disciplines of Execution*, 2nd edition, (New York: Free Press, 12 April 2016).

48   Ibid.

49   Ibid.

50   Ibid.

51   Ibid.

52   Ibid.

53   *The Matrix*, http://www.imdb.com/title/tt0133093/?ref_=nv_sr_1

54   *Chuck*, Millennium Films, IMDb.com, 5 May 2017, http://www.imdb.com/title/tt1610525/.

55   *Rocky*, Chartoff-Winkler Productions, IMDb.com, 3 December 1976. http://www.imdb.com/title/tt0075148

56   *Rocky*, http://www.imdb.com/title/tt0075148.

57   *Chuck*, http://www.imdb.com/title/tt1610525/.

58   *Pulp Fiction*, Miramax, IMDb.com, 14 December 1994, http://www.imdb.com/title/tt0110912/?ref_=ttfc_fc_tt.

59   *Sully*, Warner Bros Pictures, IMDb.com, 9 September 2016. http://www.imdb.com/title/tt3263904/

60   Ibid.

61   "The Matrix," (en.wikipedia.org: Wikipedia, Accessed 27 June 2018). https://en.wikipedia.org/wiki/The_Matrix#Development

62   *The Matrix*, http://www.imdb.com/title/tt0133093/?ref_=nv_sr_1.

63   Daniel Kahneman, *Thinking, Fast and Slow,* 1st paperback ed., (New York: Farrar, Straus and Giroux, 2013).

64   Ibid., p. 186.

65   Ibid., p. 89.

66   Ibid., p. 44.

67   Eric Schurenberg, "Nobel Laureate Daniel Kahneman on Making Smarter Decisions." (Podcast: Inc.com, Accessed 28 June 28, 2018). www.inc.com/daniel-kahneman/idea-lab-making-smarter-decisions.html

68   J. K. Nelson, S. J. Zaccaro, and J. L. Herman, "Strategic information provision and experiential variety as tools for developing adaptive leadership skills," *Consulting Psychology Journal*: Practice and Research, 62(2), (Web: APA-PsychNet.com, 2010), 131-142. http://psycnet.apa.org/record/2010-13314-006

69   Effectiveness, (Web: GoodReads.com, Accessed 28 August 2018), https://www.brainyquote.com/topics/effectiveness.

70   "How many questions did Neo ask in *The Matrix*?" Science Fiction

& Fantasy, (Web Forum: StackExchange.com, 1 July 2016, Accessed 27 June 2018). https://scifi.stackexchange.com/questions/131965/how-many-questions-did-neo-ask-in-the-matrix

71   Emily Bonnie, "Complete Collection of Project Management Statistics 2015," (Web: *wrike.com*, 7 July 2015, Accessed 15 September 2017).

72   Unless noted specifically, all Case Studies have names and details changed to protect privacy.

73   J. Kent Crawford, The Strategic Planning Office: A Guide to Improving Organizational Performance, (New York: Marcel Dekker, Inc., 2002).

74   Christy Pettey, contributor, "Don't Leave the PPM Strategy to Chance," (Web: *Gartner, Inc.*, 9 March 2017). http://www.gartner.com/smarter-withgartner/dont-leave-the-ppm-strategy-to-chance

75   "PMI's Pulse of the Profession: The High Cost of Low Performance," (PMI.org/Pulse: Project Management Institute, February 2014), 3. (http://www.pmi.org/-/media/pmi/documents/public/pdf/learning/thought-leadership/pulse/pulse-of-the-profession-2014.pdf)

76   Christy Pettey, "Don't Leave the PPM Strategy to Chance."

77   Leigh Buchanan, "How Great Entrepreneurs Think," (Web: Inc.com, 1 February 2011, Accessed 27 June 2018). https://www.inc.com/maga-zine/20110201/how-great-entrepreneurs-think.html

78   Kevin Cruze, "Zig Ziglar: 10 Quotes That Can Change Your Life," (Web: Forbes.com, November 28, 2012). https://www.forbes.com/sites/kevinkruse/2012/11/28/zig-ziglar-10-quotes-that-can-change-your-life/#4376e6a426a0

79   Jeffrey S. Welch, *BKPM Pocket Guide: For Project Managers*, (CreateSpace Independent Publishing Platform, 20 March 2015).

80   https://www.goodreads.com/quotes/1685-there-are-no-rules-here----we-re-trying-to-accomplish

81   *Halt and Catch Fire*, AMC Studios (2014-2017). https://www.imdb.com/title/tt2543312/?ref_=ttpl_pl_tt

82   Ibid.

83   "East Australian Current," (Wikipedia: Accessed 4 December 2018). https://en.wikipedia.org/wiki/East_Australian_Current

84   Ibid.

85   Ibid.

86   See "Case Study: USVantage" in Chapter 1

87   See "Case Study: Mardia" in Chapter 7

88   See "Case Study: Seeding for Change" in Chapter 7 and "Epilogue for Seeing for Change" in Chapter 8

89   See "Case Study: Pro-Fit" in Chapter 8

90   Jordan Peterson, *12 Rules for Life: An Antidote to Chaos*, (Ontario: Random House Canada, 23 January 2018).

91   See More from "We Learned a Lot" in Chapter 8.

92   Ian Needs, "Why PMOs Fail: 5 Shocking PMO Statistics," (Web: KeyedIN.com, Accessed 1 November 2018). https://www.keyedin.com/keyedin-projects/article/why-pmos-fail-5-shocking-pmo-statistics/

93   Jane, "20 Quotes to Inspire Personal Effectiveness and Self-management," (HabitsforWellbeing.com, Accessed 7 Nov 2018). https://www.habits-forwellbeing.com/20-quotes-to-inspire-personal-effectiveness-and-self-management/

94   M. E. Mullaly & J. Thomas, "Re-thinking project management maturity: perspectives gained from explorations of fit and value." Paper presented at PMI® Research Conference: Defining the Future of Project Management, (Washington, DC. Newtown Square, PA: Project Management Institute, 2010). https://www.pmi.org/learning/library/management-maturity-model-performance-assessment-6491

95   "Two-factor theory," (Wikipedia: Accessed 4 December 2018) https://en.wikipedia.org/wiki/Two-factor_theory

96   A whitepaper describing the Think Effective Assessment Model (TEAM), authored by Gruebl, Welch, and Matthews, Copyright © 2018 by Think Systems Inc., can be found at https://thinksi.com/white-paper-modernizing-the-pmo-maturity-assessment/.

97   Dan McCarthy, "The Common Traits of Successful Senior Executives." https://www.thebalance.com/characteristics-of-most-successful-senior-executives-2275904.

98   Tom DiNapoli, "Classic Movie Line #22." YouTube.com, 13 February 2008. Accessed June 27, 2018. https://www.youtube.com/watch?v=jh-dhGlsh98

99   Tony Gruebl, "5 Strategies for Delivering Bad News: Roseanne Roseannadanna, tell them the truth!" (LinkedIn.com, 17 July 2017). https://www.

linkedin.com/pulse/5-strategies-delivering-bad-news-roseanne-tell-them-tony-gruebl/

100   Gaybutton, "Wrong." YouTube.com, 15 January 2012. Accessed June 27, 2018. https://www.youtube.com/watch?v=AJLqTYAhlgk

101   Michael Bloch, et. al, "Delivering Large-Scale IT Projects On Time, On Budget, And On Value."

102   *Edge of Tomorrow.* http://www.imdb.com/title/tt1631867/?ref_=nv_sr_1

103   Ibid.

104   *Edge of Tomorrow.* http://www.imdb.com/title/tt1631867/?ref_=nv_sr_1

105   *The Matrix,* http://www.imdb.com/title/tt0133093/?ref_=nv_sr_1

106   Sun Tzu, translated by Lionel Giles, *The Art of War* (Web: Brainy-Quote.com, Accessed June 28, 2018). https://www.brainyquote.com/quotes/sun_tzu_387509

107   Tiger Woods, (Web: GoodReads.com, Accessed 27 June 2018), https://www.goodreads.com/quotes/76040-no-matter-how-good-you-get-you-can-always-get.

108   Henry Ford, (Web: GoodReads.com, Accessed 27 June2 018), https://www.brainyquote.com/quotes/henry_ford_383662.

109   Warren Buffet, (Web: GoodReads.com, Accessed 27 June 2018), https://www.brainyquote.com/quotes/warren_buffett_149691

110   *Sully.* http://www.imdb.com/title/tt3263904/

111   Tony Robbins, (Web: ExploreForAYear.com, Accessed 27 June 2018). http://exploreforayear.com/clarity/45-inspiring-quotes-change

112   *Pulp Fiction,* http://www.imdb.com/title/tt0110912/?ref_=ttfc_fc_tt

113   HabitsforWellbeing.com "20 Quotes to Inspire Personal Effectiveness and Self-management" accessed August 15, 2019, https://www.habitsforwellbeing.com/20-quotes-to-inspire-personal-effectiveness-and-self-management

114   *The Matrix,* http://www.imdb.com/title/tt0133093/?ref_=nv_sr_1

Master the Framework
TO YOUR SUCCESS

Now that you are ready to awaken your business sense to operating in a red pill world, we want you to have the tools necessary to succeed. Taking the red pill is a daily prescription not a one-time shot in the arm and so you'll need these tools to make it sticky. Allow yourself to rewire and see new things, make new connections, and develop a more holistic understanding of your operational world.

FREE Bonus Workbook

Tap into the unparalleled experience of Think Systems, Inc. C-Suite intelligence though this exclusive bonus workbook that unveils how your organization can hit the reset button on corporate culture. Register for your copy of this invaluable resource at: **www.thinksi.com/redpill**

Radically change your lens and perspective to uncover the critical role of culture in performance and effectiveness

Every project is a microcosm of how company operations, technology, and culture intersect. Open your eyes to the third dimension.

Pick the lock on the Red Pill vault and get the operational improvement and effectiveness that 20 years from now will be the new standard

*This is a limited time offer register today
Visit : thinksi.com/redpill to register for your copy .

◢think

Think Systems Inc., a Baltimore-based management consulting firm that provides on the ground technology and operations transformation, led by executives, adapted for the mid-market. If you are interested in learning more about our services visit us at thinksi.com.

CPSIA information can be obtained
at www.ICGtesting.com
Printed in the USA
JSHW020026230621
16058JS00003B/14

9 781642 799491